Practical creativity is not an oxymoron with The ChrisLin Method. In this book, Christina and Lindsey have brought creativity in thinking and practice to coaches and therapists. Whether you previously thought of yourself as creative or not, the ChrisLin Method will enable you to add this depth to your practice. They offer easy-to-follow tools and structures to encourage practitioners to use creativity to access a client's emotions and unconscious mind in a safe and supportive way.

The ChrisLin Method is the core structure, and they helpfully offer exploratory questions to use in drawing out meaning and facilitating change in the client. The book takes you through a session step by step, and the case studies bring the tools to life.

They also provide Frameworks for three common issues – Anxiety, Boundaries, and Anger. The comprehensive explanations are supplemented by case studies to show the Framework in action. I particularly appreciated that they are not formulaic in their approach but point out how the practitioner uses their expertise to choose appropriate questions to facilitate the client's learning.

For those who want a deeper understanding of the approach, they offer further reading resources, both in the relevant section and in a comprehensive bibliography. For those (like me) who want to prove the value in their practical approach to creativity, we have what we need to give it a go and introduce the ChrisLin Method into our practices.

Amanda Bouch, Leadership Coach and Team Facilitator

I wish I had a book like this when I was at the start of my career! I felt as though someone had taken me by the hand and showed me around – it has a lovely feeling and flow to it, not didactic in any way, but the sense of sharing something important and special. Almost like being asked to consider "Imagine if...."

I love how client-led the book is and the use of so many approaches but also how fluid it is and 'roomy' while still being a safe space for practitioners, full of encouragement for creativity and curiosity. So many other coaching models can put clients and coaches in boxes and be very transactional – the ChrisLin Method is generous, welcoming, and kaleidoscopic, inspiring real rhizomatic learning and insights for the client and the practitioner where both can grow and flourish in a very organic way, taking the different things they need.

There is so much to love about this book: the chapter quotes which give a flavour of what is to come, how the learning is consolidated with questions and space for reflection, and the suggested reading and myriad resources showing that this is just the start of the journey, so useful when referring back, making notes. As a practitioner there is always something new to learn. It is invaluable for practitioners who want to invite their clients to discover new awareness and resourcefulness. The case studies really show how The 5 Steps, 9 Core Questions and Frameworks work together in a very organic, synergistic and contextualised way and are not set in stone. I especially liked the Boundary Case Study.

Thank you both for sharing so much and for taking me on this exciting and inspiring journey!

Anna Gordon, Coach, Hypnotherapist, Business Coaching Psychologist

I've been on a number of ChrisLin training workshops, and I often use Christina and Lindsey's Method in my work. I loved seeing The ChrisLin Method laid out so clearly. This will be a book I refer back to again and again. I have found this method to be a 'go to' when a client is stuck with something that seems to be a mystery, as so often happens in client work. This book clearly encapsulates the process and leads the reader through step by step. Clear examples are given to bring the theory to life, leading practitioners to become confident in using these simple tools to reach clients' deeper subconscious parts.

Fiona Eaton, Integrative Counsellor, Diploma in Therapeutic Counselling (accredited)

This book is an invaluable aid to helping clients use their creativity to make shifts in their life by accessing the power of the subconscious. The ChrisLin Method is a useful simple structure to guide the coach to help clients release their creativity. Lindsey and Christina are generous with sharing their expertise and experience, which gives the practitioner confidence in using the methods.

Since reading the book I've used the ChrisLin Method to explore the shapes, colours, voices and stories in the images that clients have created in just a few minutes. I've witnessed shifts in emotion, aha moments, tears of joy and sadness, and insights that simply would not arise from traditional coaching and therapy messages.

I find it particularly useful for exploring emotions such as anger with clients, and the descriptions of the different types of anger really ring true. The case studies and examples are helpful in understanding how the process can be used. The authors offer support and advice throughout the book, and it's a 'must-read' for any practitioner looking to expand their coaching practice into the world of creativity.

Karen Kimberley, author of Thinking Like Magic, BA, DCH, DHP, NLP, GQHP, MAC, ITOL

Creativity is elusive. How can we become more creative in a fast-changing world which is demanding us to be more resourceful and experimental in how we work with each other? This is the book you have been waiting for! Christina and Lindsey have developed a how-to guide for those of you who work with clients and want to be more creative. When I read the draft I was engaged and spellbound by the ChrisLin Method. This book reveals what it takes to offer creative ways of working to your clients. Whether you are a counsellor, therapist, coach, manager, or team, you will find more than enough here to support you to structure, and develop yourself, your clients and colleagues. I thoroughly recommend this book to you and encourage you to experiment with The Method and Frameworks. Maybe attend a workshop or two. Thank you, Christina and Lindsey, for developing this book.

Dr David P Lines, PhD, Executive Coach, Founder and Director of David Lines & Associates

Creativity is a vital ingredient in our ability to change and grow – or to get unstuck. The ChrisLin Method described in this book has been developed to guide counsellors, coaches and therapists – not just to wake up their own creativity, but to facilitate clients to do the same! You will find lots of innovative and practical ideas in this well-presented book, and I recommend it to anyone involved in facilitating change.
Penny Tompkins, Psychotherapist, creator of Symbolic Modelling (using the Clean Language of David Grove), co-author of Metaphors in Mind: Transformation through Symbolic Modelling

As a coach, I have nearly a hundred books on my shelf about coaching. This reflects the fact that not all books deliver what they promise. But this one does. Having experienced Christina and Lindsey's transformational work during the existential crisis-inducing period of the first lockdown, I had some idea what to expect. I knew that this book would ignite my curiosity in a safe way. It didn't make me feel nervous about what I didn't know but instead assured me that by the end of the read, I'd know more. For me, this comes down to four things: the book's clear structure, the authors' honest language, just enough reference to academic research to reassure the cynic in me that it builds on the wisdom of others and – most importantly – a set of practical tools and techniques which I find memorable and am therefore confident to use.

I love The 9 Core Questions and the way the book unpacks these. My personal favourite is question 5 – what is in the space? Asking about emptiness can feel risky in other coaching approaches, but in a creative session, it feels completely natural. And boy does it open up new vistas! And the clincher? Those reflective questions at the end of each chapter which invariably lodge in my brain, like a little earworm, keeping me curious and deepening my knowledge of myself. Secretly, I think this is why coaches coach. Christina and Lindsey's book is, therefore, a contribution not only to the way we do the work we do with others but also with ourselves.
Shirley Collier, MBE, Executive Coach, Mentor, Consultant

Discover the ChrisLin Method by Christina Bachini and Lindsey Wheeler – a transformative system that unlocks the secrets to growing in the face of life's challenges. Their practical approach empowers you to overcome seemingly insurmountable obstacles with resilience and grace. Follow their step-by-step process to foster compassion and embrace a fresh, hopeful perspective. Whether you're seeking personal growth or helping others, the ground-breaking ChrisLin Method helps you reframe, recover and rise above, paving the way to a fulfilling and expansive life.
Carey Davidson, author of The Five Archetypes: Discover Your True Nature and Transform Your Life and Relationships

The ChrisLin Method

5 Steps for Working Creatively with Imagery & Metaphor

Christina Bachini

Lindsey Wheeler

First Published in Great Britain in 2023 by Springtime Books

© Copyright Christina Bachini and Lindsey Wheeler, 2023

All rights reserved. No part of this publication may be reproduced, stored in or introduced into a retrieval system, or transmitted, in any form, or by any means (electronic, mechanical, photocopying recording or otherwise) without the prior written permission of the publisher.

This book is sold subject to the condition that it shall not, by way of trade or otherwise, be lent, resold, hired out, or otherwise circulated without the publisher's prior consent in any form of binding or cover other than that in which it is published and without a similar condition including this condition being imposed on the subsequent purchaser.

ISBN: 978-1-915548-14-6

Cover image by Lucy Harris, Illustrator

Internal illustrations by Christian Scott, Illustrator

Disclaimer
All names in this book have been changed for reasons of client confidentiality.

Contents

	Introduction	1
1	Creativity as a Therapeutic Approach	9
2	The ChrisLin Method	17
3	Step 1: Introducing Creativity to a Client	27
4	Step 2: The Process of Creation	35
5	Step 3: Exploring the Client's Creation	45
6	Step 4: Integrating the Changes	53
7	Step 5: Closing the Session	59
8	Case Study Using The 9 Core Questions	63
9	Introducing The ChrisLin Frameworks	71
10	Framework for Working with Anxiety: Separating Imagination from Reality	75
11	Framework for Working with Boundaries: Identifying Strong and Wobbly Boundaries	87
12	Framework for Working with Anger	103
	Afterword	115
	Bibliography	117
	References	121
	Further Resources	127
	Acknowledgements	131
	About the Authors	133

Introduction

Why we wrote this book

We wrote this book because, over the course of our careers, we have used, experimented and tested many theories, models, approaches and techniques. However, in our opinion, none have been as impactful or effective in facilitating lasting change for our clients as the power of creativity. That's not to say that creativity is the only tool in our toolkit or should be in yours either – far from it. But we believe it has a significant role to play in helping clients look at their underlying, unconscious drivers that so affect their unhelpful emotions, feelings and behaviours. For this reason, we believe creativity deserves a prominent place in any practitioner's toolkit.

By practitioner we mean counsellors, coaches, art therapists and anyone engaged in delivering therapy or facilitating the personal development of others, or in training to do so. We hope that includes you, but if not, you are still very welcome here and we hope you find something of value for you personally in this book.

Over the years, we have noticed that relatively few practitioners use creativity as part of their regular practice. This is likely because many practitioners only encounter it during their training, perhaps if they are in an art therapy course or have attended one of the more progressive humanistic courses. To our mind, this is a great shame and deprives the trainee of a beneficial tool that can make an enormous difference to the client's journey. And one that can frequently shorten that journey.

Our personal charter, therefore, is to spread the word. It is to share our knowledge about the use of creativity and how powerful it can be and, by virtue of this, help clients all over the world to move on from their trauma or difficulties more quickly.

What we share here results from a willingness to consistently push our professional boundaries, experiment with creativity and refine our ideas. Through our work, research and 50+ years of collective experience, our philosophy has taken shape, and we have designed and developed what we now call 'The ChrisLin Method'.

By writing this book, we hope to encourage you to use creativity and give you the confidence to use *The ChrisLin Method* with your clients. We aim to present it in a simple and straightforward way and provide enough information so you can:

- Understand how creativity works.
- Know when to offer creativity to your clients.
- Be confident in using *The ChrisLin Method* as an intervention.
- Learn how to work with your client's creation.

Primarily, what we share in this book is based on empirical evidence from our own experiences and the results reported by other practitioners. But it is also highly influenced by our own personal approach to our work, founded in the humanistic, pluralistic and person-centred schools of thought.

> "I have no special talents. I am only passionately curious."
> **Albert Einstein** – *Physicist*

We believe *The ChrisLin Method* has therapeutic value in enabling the exploration of the hidden, unconscious depths of a client's inner world. In the following chapters, we detail *The 5 Steps* and *The 9 Core Questions* of *The ChrisLin Method* and share a case study that demonstrates the use of *The 9 Core Questions*. You will also find three different creative *Frameworks* addressing emotions that crop up regularly in the practice room: anxiety, boundaries and anger, which we hope will be helpful and inspire you to work creatively with your own clients. Our aim is to help you, the practitioner, feel confident and well-resourced to take your client on a journey of discovery.

Over time we have gathered a wonderful community of practitioners, many of whom we see time and time again on our workshops and training courses, and we want to thank you for your wisdom, support and encouragement in writing this book. Our hope is that you enjoy reading this book and gain as much pleasure and satisfaction from using *The ChrisLin Method* in your practice as we do in ours.

How we came together

We came together by a fortuitous whim.

Introduction

It was either a lucky accident or the universe matching us, depending on your point of view. Christina decided she wanted to share with other practitioners how she worked creatively with clients. Not quite knowing how this might come about, she put a message out there, 'to the universe' (by which we mean her network), asking if anyone wanted to collaborate and share ideas. Lindsey immediately responded because it perfectly matched her love of exploring new tools and models, and this proved to be the beginning of a great friendship and professional relationship.

We freely shared our knowledge and experiences and found that our passion for creativity, both with individuals and teams, developed into something very distinctive. Together we saw how easy it was for people to move through their difficulties when they externalised their inner world using a creative technique.

Over our years together, we have continued to bring our unique perspectives, expertise and knowledge into the frame and to seek new ways of helping clients get to the root of their issues. We firmly believe that the root of the issue is where the work needs to be done for long-lasting change to emerge. We have spread our knowledge and encouraged others to use creativity by sharing what we have developed with fellow practitioners through our workshops and training, and we are truly grateful that participants continue to affirm the value of this work and encourage us to do more.

Who this book is for

This book is written with counsellors, coaches and art therapists in mind, but in fact can be read by anyone in a related discipline who is curious and wants to explore and experiment with a different approach to their practice.

Sometimes this curiosity is driven by an interest in what creativity can do for clients. Sometimes it results from frustration with the practitioner's existing toolkit. Others seek new ways to improve their clients' outcomes. We also find that some practitioners are themselves creative in some way and would like creativity to be a more significant part of their lives. But this is by no means a prerequisite. Many long-standing techniques, such as sand play, have been adopted by counsellors who would not consider themselves creative in the slightest!

However you came to this book, we are confident that practitioners who learn and use *The ChrisLin Method* will be surprised at how easy it is to use and, more importantly, will be delighted with the difference it makes to their clients' journeys.

What this book has to offer

We'd like this book to be a valuable resource for you that you can delve into whenever you need inspiration or help to work creatively with your clients. As such, we hope we have written it in a way that you can drop into any chapter and find what you want. We aim to give enough information so you understand *The ChrisLin Method* and how it is applied and can become confident with the approach. Ultimately, we hope you will learn the *Method* and a suite of *Frameworks* that you are so comfortable with, you can use them interchangeably, adapt them and make them your own.

We aim to help you, the practitioners, feel confident and well-resourced to take your client on a journey of discovery

---

In the following chapters, we tell you a bit more about ourselves and our journey with creativity and reveal how to work successfully with *The ChrisLin Method*. Chapters 1-7 explain what makes creativity so powerful and introduce *The 5 Steps* and *The 9 Core Questions* that are the model's foundation. Chapter 8 provides a case study focused on using only *The 9 Core Questions* so you can see how well they work. Chapter 9 onwards unpacks three topics that we often see when working with clients: anxiety, boundary issues and anger, and we share an individual creative *Framework* for each one. Within each of these *Frameworks* we also provide a case study to bring the method alive and illustrate how you can apply *The 5 Steps* and *The 9 Core Questions*.

At the back of the book, you will find a bibliography and more information about the people and models we mention and a list of interesting resources to assist you on your creative journey.

Working with unhelpful emotions

Helping clients explore their stories is what we all hope to do as professionals. We aim to support our clients as they journey to the heart of the matter and then uncover more helpful ways of 'being' today, in the present. It is here that working creatively really comes into its own as it assists the client to bypass the conscious mind, where all the current thinking and belief is enacted, and allows them to look at the underlying beliefs and values that are really driving their behaviour.

Introduction

Through our time of working creatively with clients, we have worked with every human experience, from anger to zeal (a true perfectionist!). In our view, emotions are what give us feedback and are a necessary part of life. Emotions are a temperature gauge of how life is, what is going well and what is not. And although people can say that their unhelpful emotions are present all the time (and it can certainly feel like an emotion is a constant presence), in reality, we only notice them from moment to moment. No one can be constantly joyful, or constantly grief-stricken or angry. But our language around emotions can lead us to believe differently.

> "The psychological rule says that when an inner situation is not made conscious, it happens outside as fate."
> Carl Jung – *Psychiatrist and psychologist*

Similarly, there is a massive disparity in how people interpret their emotions and what labels they give them. What for one person is shame, someone else will call low self-esteem; what for one is anxiety, another will call fear. Whatever the label, it's essential that the practitioner listens for and accepts the client's name for their emotions and works with it. Inserting your own definition is generally not helpful and may lead to unnecessary confusion.

However, the truth is, very few clients come into a session saying they want to work on their 'emotions'. It is much more likely clients will say they feel sad a lot of the time, feel anxious, have lost their mojo or don't know where they are going in life. Most clients know something is not right but may have no idea what is causing this lack of rightness. Conversely, some may be wedded to their story and seem committed to a fixed reason for why they feel like they do but still struggle to make sense of it and express it verbally.

This inability of clients to precisely express what is going on for them is common. And it's no wonder they struggle because they are often experiencing a mash of emotions and feelings generated by their current and past life experiences and fuelled by their own responses (behaviours) to their situation. A lot is going on – at the conscious and subconscious levels.

This is where *The ChrisLin Method* can really help. Because it is through creatively exploring these unhelpful emotions that clients can untangle their thoughts. When clients are invited to work creatively, they are able to represent complex emotions and confused thinking outside of themselves. By the very act of creating a physical representation – an image, a clay model, a formation of buttons, whatever it is – they become an observer of, and to some degree disassociated from, their emotions. Their creation provides a window into their unconscious beliefs and values that are driving their current thoughts, feelings and behaviours. This window offers an opportunity to find new meaning about the issue and, ultimately, alternative ways of dealing with it.

Definition of Intuition: "Knowledge or belief obtained neither by reason nor by perception."
Collins English Dictionary

Often the client's creation can be broken down into smaller chunks, and the individual components evaluated to disclose more manageable information. Clients can also uncover where their beliefs and values have come from and, by virtue of this, start to really understand why they do what they do. With this new understanding of themselves, they can see, sometimes for the first time, options and choices open up before them and figure out how to move forward more positively.

When you work creatively with people, movement takes place

Why practitioners should use The ChrisLin Method

Since the beginning of time, people of the world have expressed themselves through art, music, dance, drama and storytelling. It is the universal way for people to communicate their thoughts, ideas, feelings and spirituality. These modes of communication are deep and meaningful, both to the 'creator' and the 'witness' of the art form.

Many of us will have had an experience of being totally moved by a piece of music, art, drama or a story being told through words or imagery about something important to the 'creator'.

Although it is the creator's own story, somehow it resonates with the witness, and their own story, in a way that they too become engaged. These stories touch us because they tap into our unconscious thoughts, feelings and emotions and bring them to the surface so that we can fully experience them, sometimes as tears, joy, fear or anger or some other emotion.

Working creatively with clients is also about working with the unconscious mind because this is where our beliefs and values are stored, created as they are from the beliefs and values of our parents, our early life, culture and life experiences. As a result, the unconscious mind is the hidden controller of our thoughts, feelings and actions.

When clients enter the room, they, and we as practitioners, are often most concerned with what their conscious mind is telling them. Much of our work is connected to helping clients gain clarity and some relief from the relentless churn of their thoughts.

It is here, we believe, that working creatively with a client is particularly helpful. With the *Methods* and *Frameworks* we describe in this book, clients are provided with a safe environment to venture into their unconscious to uncover their thinking patterns and the principles behind them.

This kind of approach will be familiar to those who have studied art therapy and perhaps to counsellors, where sand play, use of cards or other kinaesthetic interventions have been used for decades to help clients access and examine their unconscious thoughts.

However, it was through our own use of creativity that we realised how much we could all benefit from some deeper study on the actual process that takes place when we work creatively and identify a structure that would make creativity accessible as an intervention to all practitioners.

So that has been our aim, to provide a *Method* that others can follow in the knowledge that it works and can be successfully replicated in the therapy room with your own clients.

Coming up

In the first chapter we discuss creativity, exploring what it is, its long history as an intervention and what it brings to the therapeutic process of development and change. We disentangle the terms 'artistic' and 'creative' to release ourselves from the belief that we need to be an artist to work creatively. And importantly, we explore how working in this way allows the client to discover their inner world in a safe and accessible way that leads to real change.

From Chapter 2 onwards we unwrap *The ChrisLin Method* in detail to explain how and when to use it, and from Chapter 8 onwards we provide case studies and *Frameworks* to work with three specific emotions and behaviours so you can see exactly how *The ChrisLin Method* is applied. At the end of each chapter you will find additional resources on the topic under discussion to provide further learning.

A question for you

What brought you to this book? Use the space below to note what brought you here, what you are curious about and what you hope to learn.

Engaging further

Book: *The Power of Now* by Eckhart Tolle

Book: *The Art Therapy Sourcebook* by Cathy A Malchiodi

1
Creativity as a Therapeutic Approach

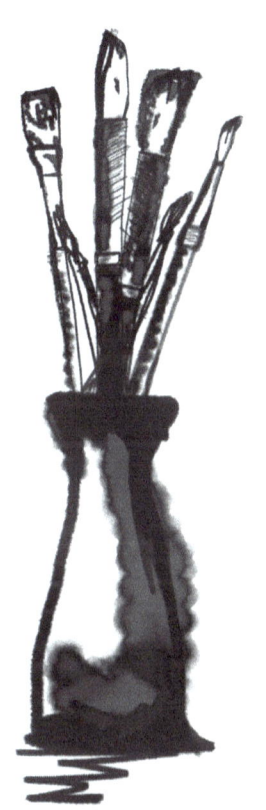

"The artist is not a special kind of person, but every person is a special kind of artist."
Ananda K Coomaraswamy
Philosopher of Indian art

Artistic vs creative

We want to start by saying we do not think of ourselves as 'artistic' people but as 'creative' people, and to our minds, there is a difference. Art is something that takes a long time to practise and become proficient in. In our view, anyone *can* be creative. In fact, we believe everyone *is* creative in some shape or form.

From gardening, home décor, the way people dress, DIY, dancing, poetry or music to the more traditional hobbies of woodworking, painting, pottery, knitting, dressmaking or quilting. Creativity shows up everywhere and most of the time it's born from a person listening to their intuition and doing what feels right to them.

Similarly, creativity in the practice room requires no artistic ability or any *particular* creative skill. It only requires an acceptance to go with the flow and a willingness to listen to the inner self.

This book explains how to help clients let go of their logical thoughts and listen to their intuition as a door to their unconscious. Once accessed and given a voice, the unconscious can share its hidden wisdom and knowledge, enabling the client to connect with their issue and discover a different perspective.

Once the client is willing and able to 'go with the flow', they can create an image, metaphor, motif or symbol representing their issue. And they can do so using any creative materials that you, as the practitioner, offer them or that they discover themselves as the 'right' medium. Sometimes the right medium is paints, sometimes pencils, sometimes it's objects from around the home or office, sometimes it's items from nature, or fabrics, or a postcard. The choices are endless, as you'll discover below.

What do we mean by creativity?

Creativity to us means any creative process! In its simplest form, it may be a person with a piece of paper and a pencil. Or it may mean a flipchart and some marker pens. It could be paints, felt tips, fabrics, collage or items like stones, petals or even the written word. It can also be music or movement. While, in general, we tend to use creative materials like pens and paper and natural items, in fact, any medium can be used as long as the client is able and willing to use the materials to represent their issue outside of themselves.

This act of externalising their difficulty creates a safe place for their hurt, trauma, or confusion to be explored, examined and, with help from the practitioner, for it to shift and move towards more positive feelings and behaviour.

We believe that when you are working with a client creatively, this is where the alchemy starts. It is through their image or creation that it becomes possible to delve deeper into the unconscious and its influence on the client's life. The search for meaning creates understanding and, ultimately, transformation and offers the creator an opportunity to transition from pain to awareness into acceptance and peace, or whatever internal state the client is striving for.

When the client uses their intuition to create their image, they are allowing the door to open into the unconscious thoughts and beliefs driving their behaviour. In this way, we give the unconscious a voice that can be heard and worked with.

Just as there are many creative activities that people indulge in, there are an equal number of creative approaches that can be used in the practice room. Some of the more common ones are listed below. But really, there are no creative limits to representing the client's inner world.

Examples of creative materials

- Colouring pencils
- Felt tips
- Paints
- Fabric
- Crafting supplies, e.g., stickers, motifs
- Postcards
- Angel cards, Archetype cards
- Photographs
- Nature – leaves, twigs, petals, feathers
- Food items – dried pasta, seeds, pulses
- Items found on a desk or table
- Flipchart or whiteboard
- Magazine images
- Bags of buttons, Lego bricks or a random collection of small items
- Stones or pebbles

We explain more about how to introduce creativity to clients and the use of creative materials later in the book, and in Chapter 8 onwards we give practical examples of how to work creatively with clients.

Representing the client's inner world

Fiction writers sometimes speak about a book writing itself. They had an outline plan for the book, but once they started writing, the characters wrote the story. The author had no idea where the story was going and expressed surprise about the twists and turns it took.

The unconscious mind is the hidden controller of our thoughts, feelings and actions

---

Using creativity and facilitating the client to create images is a similar process. When the cognitive part of the brain takes a rest and lets the unconscious do its job, the creation of a physical 'model' or representation of the client's inner world is free to come into being.

This is always a helpful exploration, particularly when the client seems to be lost for words, finding it difficult to articulate what they feel, or if the practitioner senses that there is something deeper going on that it would be helpful to explore.

These moments of creativity enable the client to externally represent their inner world, where it is safe to explore, question and delve to uncover hidden depths. In doing so, clients find new perspectives and can view their issues differently, and practitioners can better understand the pathway the client is on. There is always movement, a learning, a realisation, a discovery to be made that helps the client on their journey. Even if this discovery is that they are not yet ready to move forward.

Creativity as a Method

Creativity as a therapeutic approach has a long history, including the work of Adrian Hill, often considered the founder of art therapy in the UK, and the work of Margaret Naumburg and Edith Kramer in the USA in the 1940s. Even earlier, Freud had made connections between imagery and the unconscious mind. And Carl Jung's views on the importance and value of understanding one's 'inner city' is still foundational to understanding the human condition. More recently, the benefits and outcomes of creativity as a therapeutic approach have been deeply researched and documented. If you are interested in this research, much of it is listed in the bibliography on the American Art Therapy Association website.

It houses specific research concerning aspects of working creatively with different groups of people, different forms of abuse, trauma, disease, addiction, mental illness and much more.

> "The creative process, so far as we are able to follow it at all, consists in the unconscious activation of an archetypal image, and in elaborating and shaping this image into the finished work. By giving it shape, the artist translates it into the language of the present, and so makes it possible for us to find our way back to the deepest springs of life."
> **Carl Jung** – *Psychiatrist and psychologist*

In our formative years and during our early life experiences (as well as later life experiences), we adopt beliefs, values, moral parameters, rituals and much more from our environment. We learn to adapt ourselves to fit in, stay safe and be accepted and loved. These early mechanisms become automatic responses that we do without much conscious thought, which is where the problem may lie. We appear to just 'know' how to be, what to do and what to say based on information that was often laid down when we were young. However, what worked when we were young or in a particular situation may not be what a person would choose if this unconscious baggage were not the backseat driver.

That's not to say the unconscious cannot be trusted. It does many valuable things for us and has a positive purpose. Often, at the root of it, it aims to keep us safe and protected and provide the best opportunity for us to achieve a sense of belonging and love. But how it goes about this may no longer work or be a useful approach.

The unconscious mind also affects how we physically feel. It is easy to see the relationship between our mind and our body when we think of situations when we just 'know' something's not quite right, or if a situation is not safe, or we get a sense that someone is lying. We notice that bodily feeling, but it's hard to define and often lurks on the edge of our conscious minds and most times we go out of our way to ignore it. Nonetheless, we know there is hidden knowledge there that is as yet untapped.

The ChrisLin Method raises this unconscious hidden knowledge to the conscious mind, helping clients notice it, understand it and feel it. In doing so, often for the first time, clients realise they have the opportunity to evaluate how the unconscious drivers influence their life and how helpful, or otherwise, they are. From this perspective, they can see they have choices to develop a more helpful approach that will serve them better.

The most common comment we hear from practitioners after learning *The ChrisLin Method* is how surprised they are at how quickly, and how deeply, their client goes when they explore their creation. In many cases, practitioners and clients alike say that they would never have reached the real root of the issue, or it would have taken much longer to reach this level of understanding without *The ChrisLin Method*. This is because the work that takes place between practitioner and client is transformative and powerful. Powerful enough to enable clients to unravel years, if not decades, of self-loathing, disruptive or self-sabotaging behaviour.

In the next few pages, we describe *The ChrisLin Method* and how it works and explain how to use it with your own clients.

What makes it so powerful?

The ChrisLin Method provides a key that can unlock thinking and enable a new kind of conversation to take place that does not rely solely on the client's ability to articulate what's going on for them or find the right words.

The image, metaphor or symbol becomes the arena where the change occurs

---

As the client's inner information is translated into some physical form, it is processed by everyone (the creator and the witness – client and practitioner) as an enabler to help move ideas forward so that a change in the thinking system can occur.

For example, if someone says, "I'm feeling completely blocked, I really don't know what to do," asking them to create the 'block' in a physical form results in the mental freedom for movement to take place. By simply creating an image of the block, the block itself is already transformed. And further investigation through skilled questioning will lead to an even greater understanding that will help reshape or dispel the block and create an opportunity for the mental shift that needs to take place.

Coming up

In the next chapter we discuss how we developed *The ChrisLin Method* and explain in detail *The 5 Steps* and *The 9 Core Questions* that can be used in all creative sessions. We break down each of the *Steps* for you so you can see the rationale behind them and how to move through them easily. We describe in detail each of the *Core Questions* and explain how to use them and why we believe it is essential you ask them in the way we recommend.

Summary

Creativity as a therapeutic approach has a long history. Extensive research is available on the benefits and outcomes.

The ChrisLin Method can be used with any client but is especially helpful when a person seems lost for words, finding it difficult to articulate what is going on. Or if the practitioner senses there is something deeper, the *Method* can be helpful for exploring in a gentle and safe way.

It is a powerful process because a creative, physical expression of an unhelpful emotion taps into the deeper levels of human consciousness and provides a mechanism to translate internal experience and information into something that can be seen and challenged.

Everyone can be creative, and no artistic ability is needed – neither the client nor the practitioner needs to be artistic.

Creative materials include pencils to paints, nature to writing, postcards to buttons, and everything in between.

Through the client's creation, it becomes possible to delve deeper into the knowledge and wisdom of the unconscious mind.

The ChrisLin Method can enable clients to unravel years, if not decades, of self-loathing, disruptive or self-sabotaging behaviour.

Engaging further

See the bibliography of research on the American Art Therapy Association website

Book: *Conscious Creativity: Look, Connect, Create* by Philippa Stanton

A question for you

What else do you need to know or understand in order to be more open to using creativity in your practice?

2
The ChrisLin Method

"Images helped clients understand, express, contain, and soothe emotions. Images also could be used behaviourally or cognitively, and they could aid in tracking client growth and progress in therapy."
Lisa Hinz
Associate Professor of Art Therapy, Dominican University of California

Development of the Method

In 2018, after a lot of discussion and sharing of our love of working creatively with clients, we realised we had great synergy and a lot in common. And we knew we wanted to spread our passion. We put together some workshops to share our knowledge and offered them face-to-face as CPD (Continuing Professional Development) for practitioners in a beautiful location by the River Thames in Berkshire.

We discovered very early on just how engaged people became in the use of creativity when given the opportunity. And this applied to all disciplines – from psychologists to coaches, art therapists to counsellors, HR managers, line managers and anyone interested in working differently with people or for their own personal development. Regardless of their initial reason for being there, everyone underwent a change that helped them in their personal and professional journey.

In a day's programme, we had time to introduce several ways of working and for people to experience them fully. An important part of this was coming together as a group after each experience, discussing what had just happened, and sharing our learning. But one of the greatest joys of working face-to-face was just being in a room with people absorbed in their work, in the knowledge they will leave having made a discovery, gained an insight and learnt something revelatory about themselves and the techniques we teach. As a group, we created a special kind of energy within a nurturing, safe space where it was okay to experiment, to be present, to drift, to learn and to be there for each other.

This face-to-face work, and the wonderful locations we had, enabled us to include outdoor experiences that showed how it's possible to work creatively with the natural world and provided reflective spaces away from the confines of a room. We also introduced techniques you can only really do in person, such as working with buttons as a form of Gestalt/ Constellation work. We used piles of colourful fabrics to physically build representations of strong and wobbly boundaries so people could really feel what it's like when someone walks into their space.

Intuition is the door to their unconscious

During this time, we documented the questions of *The ChrisLin Method*, primarily for participants who were new to creativity, to help them stay focused on the creation before them. Staying focused on the client's image or creation is probably one of the greatest challenges to anyone new to our work.

It sometimes feels strange and a bit clunky asking questions of the image or creative piece. But that is the whole point of *The ChrisLin Method*. It is our belief and assumption that there is something helpful and, as yet, unheard or unnoticed by the client that the image of their inner world can offer. Certainly, participants in the workshops found it reassuring to have pre-prepared questions to get them started when working in pairs or triads. And it ensured their focus was specifically directed towards the piece of work their fellow participant had just created.

Could we work with clients virtually?

In 2020 things changed because we could no longer offer face-to-face workshops, and we had to say goodbye to our space by the river. However, we wanted to continue working with our private clients as well as fellow practitioners. We talked a lot about the difference between working face-to-face and if and how we could work online. It was a challenging time. In fact, it's probably fair to say it was a challenging time for everyone in our profession. Could we work with clients virtually? And how could we work with them creatively?

As with many things in life, something that seems to be an obstacle at first can have a silver lining. The COVID-19 pandemic necessitated a different way of thinking, which meant we needed to adapt our approach to work with our clients and continue teaching our workshops online. We had to find new ways of engaging, introducing and explaining *The ChrisLin Method* without losing any of the experiential quality of the face-to-face work. Interestingly, although daunting at the time, the whole process was far more straightforward than we could imagine. We continue to be fascinated by the fact that working creatively online is as meaningful an experience as working face-to-face.

To date, we have worked with thousands of clients and practitioners worldwide using *The ChrisLin Method* and continue to hear what a significant difference it has made to people's lives. We are still delighted when practitioners say, "How can 10 minutes working with my client's image take them so deep, so quickly?"

Eventually, we hope to offer face-to-face workshops again because of the extra dynamic they bring and the scope we have to experience and experiment together.

What is The ChrisLin Method?

The *ChrisLin Method* is a therapeutic *Framework* with 5 distinct *Steps* and a set of *9 Core Questions*.

The 5 Steps

The 5 Steps provide the practitioner with a simple structure that leads the client from first engagement through to the embodiment of the change and the decision of what to do next with their creation. The structure is the backbone of the process and guides practitioners through the ebb and flow of the therapeutic journey. Below we briefly explain the *Steps*, and we discuss them in more detail in Chapter 3. Following the *Steps* sequentially ensures a well-run session and will boost your confidence to offer creativity as a regular part of your practice.

The key elements for each Step are:

Step 1. Introducing creativity to a client

Identify when to suggest to your client that they create something to symbolise the issue they are working on. Often it is about recognising when the client is stuck, unable to verbalise their emotions or their thinking, and would benefit from being taken away from their logical, rational brain. Sometimes the client's use of language, and regular use of metaphors, can give a clue that working creatively would be a good approach for them.

Gain buy-in to experiment with creativity by suggesting it might provide more insights into their issue.

Help clients understand that this is not about being an artist or having any artistic abilities.

Step 2. The process of creation

Remind the client that the work they will do is about slowing down, tuning into their intuition and being able to doodle or create an abstract, representation, symbol or metaphor.

Encourage the use of any creative materials, colours or shapes that they feel drawn to.

Set a time limit, such as 10 to 12 minutes, and stay silent while the client is creating. Very quickly, the client becomes absorbed. Witnessing the creation often gives the practitioner insights into the change of energy as it takes place. For instance, breathing, facial expressions and movement are all clues as to what is happening for the client.

Step 3. Exploring the client's creation

The practitioner listens to the client's story of their creation and also notices the image as a whole and its component parts.

Use all or some of *The 9 Core Questions* to encourage and guide the client to dig deeper into the image and uncover what it has to offer.

Once exploration and change have occurred, ask if the client wants to add or remove anything from the image to represent the change that has taken place. Sometimes people want to create an entirely new image; sometimes they are content to add or take things away.

Step 4. Integrating the changes

Up to this point, all the work has happened outside of the client, and it is likely you will see physical as well as mental shifts in the person. You may notice an intake of breath, a smile, relaxing back into their chair, a scratching of the head or a furrowed brow.

Integration happens by supporting the client to embody the change. For example, suggest they pick up their image, hold it to their heart and breathe it in. Or ask the client to project out into the future and notice how they can behave differently.

This concludes the creative process.

Step 5. Closing the session

When the client is out of the creative process, check they have achieved what they set out to achieve. It may be a complete shift and therefore the process is complete, or a smaller shift that lets the client know there has been a change, but there may be more work to do.

Ask the client what they want to do with their creative piece. Do they want to take it home and have it on view? Do they need to perform a ritual with it? For instance, safely burn it, tear it up or bury it in the garden? The client needs to make their own decision and will usually have a clear idea.

Some clients may want to leave their image with the practitioner. Leaving the image with you does not mean you can dispose of it. They may wish to refer to it again in the future. If appropriate, when they book their final session, you can remind them you have it in safekeeping and that you only keep client notes for a short period of time.

The 9 Core Questions

The questions we outline below and delve into in much more detail in Chapter 4 are specifically designed to guide the client through the exploration of their creation and reach some new level of understanding about themselves.

When clients seem wholly mystified by their image, it takes patience and encouragement to tease out meaning

---

It is important to realise that *The 9 Core Questions* are written for an ideal situation with a client willing to experiment and fully engage in the experience. But, as you know, there is never a scenario where you can just roll out a textbook technique! The task is to understand the purpose of the flow so you can be client-led and flexible with how you apply the Method.

During a client session, the practitioner must use their own judgement about the need for each question and may choose to spend more or less time with each one or circle back and ask a question again. A lot will depend on the client. A question like "Tell me the story of your image" can produce very different responses. Some clients will do a lot of the work and explain what each colour, texture and shape means to them. (In our vocabulary, the unconscious mind is ready and willing to 'come out to play' and reveal what has been hidden.) This means you can focus on asking questions about the parts they do not mention; for example, the space that's left empty or the relationship between components. In other cases, the client seems wholly mystified by their image, and it takes patience and encouragement to tease out meaning – their unconscious can be hiding somewhere pretty deep – and it may take a little while for the client to connect with what is in their creation.

Over the years, we have researched many questions and tested their sequencing with many clients and practitioners to identify the ones that help clients to do the following:

- Uncover their unconscious drivers.
- Understand the purpose of their unconscious drivers – how they were helping to support the client.
- Develop choices about how, or if, these drivers should continue to influence the client.

The *Core Questions* are used within *Step 3: Exploring the Client's Creation*. To us, it's important that the questions have a forward momentum, by which we mean they create a positive shift and provide a route to a new way of being, and don't stop at identifying what is going 'wrong'.

By following the *Core Questions*, you are assured of providing your client with the space and opportunity to hear what their unconscious has to offer. This is where the learning is. The answers from this set of questions awaken the client to what is behind their thoughts and actions. From this place, with all their new understanding about themselves, the client can see options about how they can move forward and show up differently in the world. They can identify steps that lead to greater control and mastery of their lives and choose to let go of 'stuck thinking' and beliefs that are no longer helpful. A client who was once lively and gregarious but got shut down through bullying is able to remember that they still have this gregarious person inside and can creatively start to reconnect with this part of themselves.

With practice, you will learn to 'trust the process' and ask questions about every single component in the client's creation, and we urge you to use your skill and intuition to know when something important has been uncovered.

This set of questions can be used in any creative session and will ensure a thorough exploration of the creative piece and the unconscious values and beliefs that were previously hidden from the client.

The 9 Core Questions that you will use when discussing your client's work are:

1. Tell me the story of your image.
2. What does this colour represent to you?
3. What does this shape mean for you?
4. What's important about the size of this?
5. What is in the space(s)?
6. What is the relationship between this and that?
7. If this image had a voice, what would it say?
8. What does the image know now that it didn't know before?
9. Is there anything you need to add or take away from the image to represent the change that has happened?

Do I need to use all the Questions?

In short, no! Once you are familiar with the questions, you will be able to select questions based on the client in front of you and the topic they are working on. However, we strongly recommend that you spend enough time with questions 1-6 of the *Core Questions* to ensure the client has adequately explored their creation and had the opportunity to consider what it can teach them.

In Chapter 8's case study, you can read an example of when we used *The 9 Core Questions* in an actual session so you can see how well it works. In Chapters 9-11 we discuss anxiety, boundaries and anger and provide a *Framework* for working with each. These *Frameworks* include specific questions that supplement the *Core Questions* along with details of a particular creative approach to the topic.

Coming up

In the following chapters, we provide much more detail on each of *The 5 Steps*, and in *Step 1* we explain the role of the practitioner and how to introduce creativity to a client. Anecdotally this is the biggest hurdle for most practitioners who are new to this kind of work. We also discuss the possible challenges you may face and offer some advice about preparing to work with creative materials.

Summary

We have developed *The ChrisLin Method* through empirical evidence from working with thousands of clients and practitioners worldwide.

It is our belief and assumption that there is something helpful and as yet unheard or unnoticed by the client that the image of their inner world can offer.

The ChrisLin Method comprises *The 5 Steps* and *The 9 Core Questions*.

Frameworks provide a unique creative approach and supplementary questions for the topic they address.

The case studies in Chapter 8 onwards demonstrate the use of the *Core Questions* and *Framework Questions*.

Engaging further

Book: *Metaphors in Mind: Transformation Through Symbolic Modelling* by James Lawley and Penny Tompkins

Book: *Feel the Fear and Do It Anyway* by Susan Jeffers

A question for you

Having read about *The ChrisLin Method*, which of your clients would benefit most from a creative approach and when will you try it?

3
Step 1: Introducing Creativity to a Client

"But your vision will become clear only when you can look into your own heart. Without, everything seems discordant; only within does it coalesce into unity. Who looks outside dreams; who looks inside awakes."
Carl Yung
Psychiatrist and psychologist

The role of the practitioner

The role of the practitioner is to first create a safe place for themselves. A place to practice, free from a need to perform or prove expertise and with a sense of curiosity and willingness to be at one with the client, in their world.

The second is to hold the space for the client without judgement. This will come naturally to many practitioners, but it's particularly important with *The ChrisLin Method*. The practitioner must also hold the space for exploration without interpreting the client's creative work.

When working with *The ChrisLin Method*, the practitioner witnesses and assists in the exploration of the creative piece so the client can unravel, name and explain what they have created. This process opens up new depths that help the client and practitioner discover more about the topic and the behaviours, feelings, memories and reactions accompanying it. Using *The ChrisLin Method* can also help to identify the root of the behaviour – when and how it came into being – which can be incredibly illuminating.

Accept the privilege that someone has opened their inner world to you

---

Assisting the client to find the moment when they first acted in this way helps them realise there is an explanation for their belief, value or behaviour, and it becomes more apparent that their response served a purpose at some time in their life. The purpose may have been a need to be loved, belong or please, or even a need to survive.

On reaching this point, it's then possible for the client to evaluate the impact of that belief, value or behaviour in their life today, and whether it's still helpful to them.

Understanding the mechanism of what started the behaviour can provide enough of an emotional release that healing can begin to take place. After the real and felt sense has been externalised and evaluated, movement can now connect the mind, body and spirit so that a long-lasting shift can take place.

While it's possible for clients to make considerable strides in one session, they will likely need to continue to explore their creation over several sessions. Ensuring clients are not rushed and have enough time to fully understand their creation is an integral part of the process.

Often, between sessions, clients will process what has been revealed, and their thoughts will move on, so they return to the next session with new insights. Here the practitioner needs to be nimble enough to keep up with the client's thinking journey and can support them by encouraging deeper work on the existing image by unpicking its components in more detail. Or the practitioner (or client) may notice a newly emerging theme that demands its own image and investigation.

"Should I offer creativity to every client?" we hear you ask. It depends! Some practitioners choose only to work this way and use creativity with every client, or at least most of them. For the majority, though, including ourselves, *The ChrisLin Method* is another inspired option in our toolkit to be used when it seems it would be the most helpful intervention for a particular client. And surely, one of the greatest joys of being a practitioner is knowing that you have applied your craft well and helped another human being understand themselves better so they can live a more authentic and contented life.

How to introduce creativity to a new or established client

In our experience, introducing creativity to a client is much easier if you have already experienced *The ChrisLin Method* as a practitioner. Engaging someone else is much easier when you can talk about something you have personally experienced. Your energy and belief will show through, not as a persuasive mechanism, but as a way of letting your client know that you are comfortable with what you are about to embark on together and confident that a positive shift will occur.

The more naturally you introduce creativity, the better. For example, saying, "How would you like to try something different that I think may help?" or, "I think that words are getting in the way of what you need to work on. I'd like to suggest something different," will gently introduce the idea. Experiment with phrases of your own and rest assured that almost all clients will be curious and say "Yes!"

Making sure that the client knows this is not an art exam or anything you will judge or interpret is essential. Let the client know this is about free expression; there is no right or wrong, and no artistic skill is needed. Sharing that having artistic skills can actually get in the way may be helpful. This is because artistic people tend to want to create a beautiful piece of work that looks like 'something', whereas the work we ask the client to do sets aside preconceived ideas and flows freely from their intuition.

Introducing creativity can bring a gasp from the client, followed by, "I am not creative," or, "I don't have a creative bone in my body." To our mind, everyone is creative in their own unique way, and as long as they can make marks on a page, they can be encouraged to be creative in the therapy room.

Once you ask them if they can hold a felt tip pen and make lines and squiggles or just doodle, they generally relax, saying, "Yes, of course I can." It is not uncommon for people to simultaneously show excitement and resistance as they fear being inadequate or judged but are also curious about what it might reveal. So it's beneficial to offer reassurance and confirm that this is not about creating a work of art, and for you to relax and remember that this is just a normal part of settling the client into the idea.

However, practitioners must remember that this is an offering to the client rather than something everyone wants to engage in. So, if you receive much resistance, move on and offer something else.

Clients say, "I'm just not creative. I can't draw."

As we mentioned above, to be a creator of their experience, the client needs to realise that this is not about creating a piece of 'art'. It is about the ability to put some squiggles, lines, dots or dashes onto a piece of paper. It does not have to look like an object or anything recognisable. It could be, and often is, abstract with no perceivable shape or form.

The client can glue pictures or objects onto paper and use paints, pencils, fabrics or other things to represent what is going on for them. And, of course, although colour may enhance the image, it is not obligatory. A simple pencil or pen is fine because black-and-white images can still produce a deep and meaningful experience. If the client is encouraged to use their intuition and put their inner critic aside and just let the image emerge, new understanding, perspective and options will surface from the unconscious.

Once they share their image with a practitioner (a 'witness') who is curious and enquiring, they are transported to somewhere inside themselves and start to open up about what each line, dot or squiggle means for them. Very often, the client is not aware of the meaning or their thoughts when they are creating their image, but through careful questioning, their awareness grows. A simple question such as "If that part of your image had a voice, what would it say?" allows their unconscious to speak, through which the client reaps a whole new level of understanding. Most clients are astonished at how much information is encoded in their image.

From the feedback we regularly receive, clients are always amazed at how deep and meaningful the experience has become for them without them either intending or realising that this would happen.

"I had no idea I was carrying around so much stuff just under the surface waiting to grab me."
Louis, client, London

Contracting with your client

At this point, it is also helpful to talk with your client about contracting.

As we mentioned earlier, suggesting to clients that they work creatively is just an invitation to do so. And, just as you may suggest to a client that they do homework, read positive statements at night or keep a journal, the client can agree or choose not to participate. To our mind, this act of invitation is part of the ongoing contracting process. With clients who may seem reluctant, and you have space in your therapy room, you can lay out an enticing array of creative materials, and if you notice the client showing interest, you can engage them. However, suppose a client, through uncertainty, refuses to participate. In that case, it is essential to respond without judgement and say, "It was an offer, and if you don't feel you want to participate at this time, that is perfectly okay," and move on.

Some practitioners like to let clients know 'up front' they may be offering creativity as part of their practice, and this message is evident in their marketing, intake forms and written and verbal contracting. This approach can draw clients to you who are attracted to the proposition of working creatively on their topics. However, there really is no right or wrong as long as you and the client are clear on the expectations of one another.

Who provides the creative materials?

This really depends on the circumstances. For example, if you are working online with a client you may like to say that in the next session, with their permission, you'd like to introduce creativity as a way of helping them understand more about their topic. This way, it is easy enough to ask the client to gather some pens, pencils, paints or any other creative material before the next session, including some paper to work with. You can even suggest they visit a hobby craft store or raid their children's creative materials; most children have crayons, paints, felt tips, or even Play-Doh.

If you're working face-to-face, you can have your collections of creative materials on display or keep them under wraps until you are ready to work with them. The choice is yours. If you lay out the items on a table or desk, the client can sort through what they want to use. Just doing this activity can get their creative juices flowing.

In-person work has some advantages in that the client can make larger creations or use a wider range of materials, and you can even choose to walk outside together. Some things like sand trays, mask work, using Russian dolls and working with buttons are easier face-to-face, but even then, not essential. There are now online sand tray tools, masks can be drawn on a piece of paper (it works just as well), buttons can be stuck down, and other items can be sent by post.

We certainly know practitioners who send their clients a little kit in the post to get them started. Clients are generally excited to receive it and to work with the materials – although this once backfired when a client was horrified with the idea once they saw the kit! But that didn't stop them from engaging creatively; they found objects in their home that worked for them.

When we say 'creativity', we include drawing, painting, collage, mask work, storytelling, movement, music and song, as well as using props like scarfs, mirrors, postcards, bits of fabric or magazines, thread, glitter, gems, stones, shells, twigs, pinecones and anything found in the natural world. And remember, as we mentioned above, a client may have an object, or objects, from home that represents something for them, for which *The ChrisLin Method* would work just as well. For example, they may find a treasured picture at home that they are drawn to at that point in their work.

There are no limitations on where and how you can work

We have worked with clients outside, on walks, and asked them to collect things they are drawn to as they go along or to find something that represents part of their story. Clients come back with bark, leaves, feathers, petals, sticks and stones and can successfully use these to create an image on the ground or on a bench, from which we can start applying *The 5 Steps* and *The 9 Core Questions*. We have also used *The ChrisLin Method* with a photo that the client took of a scene that really spoke to them.

There are no limitations on where and how you can work. We've met corporate clients in their offices and easily used whiteboards and flip charts or their desk paraphernalia to create their stories. We have also worked in coffee shops (but only if you can find a quiet space that means clients can remain safe and secure and cannot be overheard or seen). Here we've used salt and pepper pots, sachets of tomato and mayo, and packets of sugar and salt, along with cutlery. Clients can create a whole story from how they select and place items to represent the topic they are working on. One client we worked with was having a problem with certain members of the team and used items from the table to represent each of the six members of the team using sauce, salt and pepper and sugar sachets and laid them out as a plan of the relationships. The client was able to recognise there was a distance between him and certain members of the team. By looking at the visual representation he was able to explore why the interactions were difficult with some people and what he needed to do to bridge the gap and build a more trusting team dynamic. What the client realised was that he easily built relationships with some team members who were like him and was less accepting of people who operated differently. This key insight enabled him to look at his part in the issue and develop some new strategies for how to work more effectively and bring the team together.

Creative materials can take many forms, and neither we as practitioners nor the client should be constrained by thinking of just paints, pens and pencils. At the back of the book, we provide a list of ideas and further resources. If you're still curious about how to use some of the ideas and items above, we say more about this on *The ChrisLin Method* training course.

Coming up

In the next chapter we explain *Step 2: The Process of Creation* and how to listen and look for clues that working creatively might be a good intervention for your client. We detail the verbal and physical metaphors to look out for and what to do if the client seems unable to start creating. We discuss the importance of holding the space while the client works and how to identify when the client has finished.

Summary

The role of the practitioner is to first create a safe place for themselves. A place to be free from a need to perform or prove expertise.

The practitioner's role is also to invite the client to work creatively, appropriately contract with them, put the client at ease and ensure the client knows they do not need to be artistic.

Be prepared to be curious, listen without judgement or interpretation and willing to be at one with the client in their world, which means being nimble enough to keep up with the client's thinking journey.

You and the client can contribute to the creative toolbox.

Engaging further

Book: *Drawing on the Right Side of the Brain* by Betty Edwards

Book: *Presence: Exploring Profound Change in People, Organisations and Society* by Peter Senge et al.

A question for you

Thinking about all the creative material we have mentioned here or in the list at the back of the book, what will you put into your creative kit to get you started?

4
Step 2: The Process of Creation

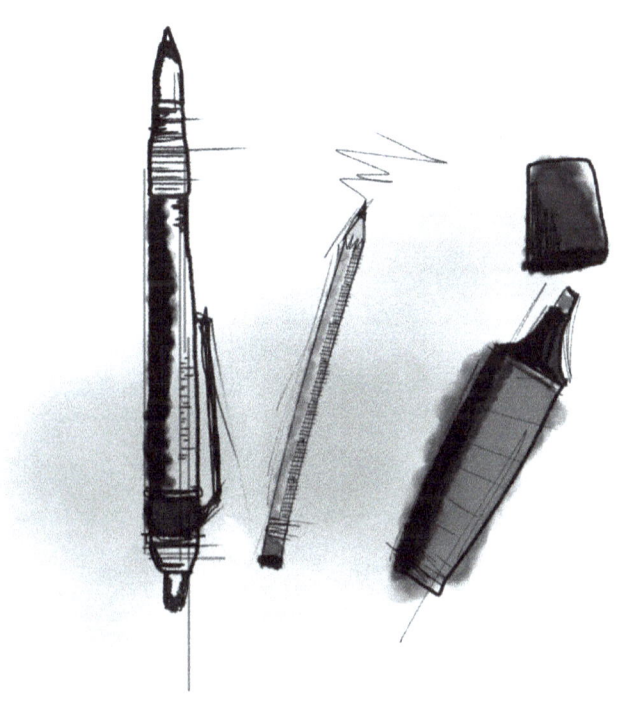

"Creativity requires the courage
to let go of certainties."
Erich Fromm
Social psychologist and philosopher

Finding a topic or metaphor to work with

Generally, the quickest way into creative work is to ask the client to centre themselves on the topic they want to work on and allow the client to talk about what's going on for them. The role of the practitioner is to notice when a metaphor, limiting belief or descriptive phrase is being used to represent their situation.

Even with clients who are unable to find the right words to fully explain their issue and what they are thinking, within their narrative, they will give clues as to their inner world and system of thinking regarding the topic. Phrases such as "He makes me so mad – it makes me boil" tell us about the feelings associated with the issue and where it might be held in the body. Remember, you may be assuming that it is their blood that is boiling, but your client may be boiling in their head. All you know is that somewhere inside of them is "makes me boil". This is helpful information to work with, and questions such as "Whereabouts is 'boil'?" and "What is 'boil' like?" will help the client engage further with their metaphor.

"And that's like what?"

The question "And that's like what?" is inspired by the Clean Language questions developed by David Grove, and it will almost always generate an answer that is a metaphor. "It's molten lava waiting to explode!" is a great response because the client is now entirely 'associated' with a metaphor and will be able to work with it during the creative activity.

As a practitioner, you are watching for moments when the client seems to be struggling to explain themselves and listening for words and phrases that you can bring to the client's attention so they are ready to move easily into creative work.

Verbal metaphors

As mentioned earlier, during your session with your client it is beneficial to purposefully listen to the client's verbal language (and watch their body language) to give you signals for whether their issue would benefit from a creative intervention.

While the client is talking about their topic, they will already be telling you what is going on for them and how it makes them feel or behave, using well-known metaphors. For instance: "Life is a battle at the moment." Such metaphors are a shorthand, an abbreviated way of explaining something complex. The problem is we all assume that we have successfully communicated something by using a metaphor without explicitly needing to discuss its context or complexity.

Sometimes the metaphor is such a common phrase that, unless we listen hard for it, we will miss it entirely. As a result, we practitioners rarely stop to challenge and check its meaning. And the client does the same – they almost certainly will have yet to unravel the meaning behind their choice of metaphor. This is very exciting because there is a considerable amount of information locked up within their words that, with the practitioner's help, the client can unpick and learn from.

Common metaphors

- There's a brick wall between us
- There's a huge mountain to climb
- My head is foggy
- It's tight across here (indicating the chest)
- I've got a weight on my shoulders
- I can't speak – I've lost my voice
- Life is a battle
- I'm stuck
- I can't speak up
- I'm trapped

We all know that there is no physical brick wall, or a mountain to climb. We understand that the head is not actually foggy, nor is there a weight on the shoulders. However, by being curious about a 'brick wall', you will almost certainly be surprised by the client's description and all the emotions and meaning they associate with it.

Body language cues

Similarly, body language cues can indicate to the practitioner that something is worth investigating. Clients will sometimes show you by their posture or hand or foot movements that something is going on physically as well as emotionally for them. For instance, the client can look weighed down by how they are sitting. They might rub their neck or stomach or use their hands in a particular way. They might have a repetitive mannerism such as squinting or fiddling with hair or swinging a leg. The practitioner can use these cues to offer the client insights, such as, "I notice when you talk about this topic, your shoulders drop in a particular way." This information may help the client to notice that they are indeed carrying a 'heavy burden'.

Another example might be when a client clutches their throat and says, "It feels like it's stuck here." The client may well be feeling a tightening in their throat as a physical response to the unhelpful emotion they are experiencing. This is a potential opportunity to work with the client creatively by asking them to create 'stuck here'.

Being a witness, just sitting quietly, unobtrusively holding a safe space, can give you many insights into the client's relationship with their topic. Their body language tells a thousand stories, and you can even pick this up during online work.

Reflecting the client's words

Reflecting back, respecting and using the client's words exactly, is a well-known technique and was identified as a counselling skill by American psychologist Carl Rogers. It is also used as an approach in the Clean Language model. It works very well in conjunction with *The ChrisLin Method* where you might repeat a whole sentence or just a word or two from what you have just heard. This has the benefit of confirming to the client that you have been attentively listening, and arguably more importantly, allows the client to hear what they just said, which offers them an opportunity to check and acknowledge their own thinking.

Names and labels

"Sticks and stones may break my bones, but words shall never hurt me"

If only this old proverb were true!

In the Introduction we spoke about the labels that practitioners and clients give emotions, feelings and behaviours, and we suggested that it is best to work with the client's name for whatever it is they are experiencing. And this is true.

But it is necessary to apply some caution because it's possible for labels to have a limiting or even negative impact.

Clients and practitioners can become locked into a label that prevents them from thinking differently. Over time, this can have an insidious effect on a client's beliefs about themselves and their identity, as well as limit the practitioner's thinking. While this may seem like nitpicking, we believe the language the client uses and hears can have a detrimental effect if not challenged by the practitioner from time to time. For example, a client taking on the identity of the emotion 'I'm a very angry person' can leave no room for anything else unless appropriately confronted.

Similarly, while many people will feel relieved to be given a label for being neurodivergent or anxious, these names can become something that people hide behind and can become the reason why people say they cannot do things, cannot change or cannot get on with their lives in the way they wish. In *some* situations, the label can become an irrefutable statement or create a defeatist frame of mind that may benefit from careful challenging.

So how and when are labels helpful? They can be useful as a personal shorthand when thinking about a client and determining an approach or intervention to use. For example, it is helpful to notice that when a client says they cannot speak up in meetings for fear of making a fool of themselves, there may be something going on with 'imposter syndrome' or 'self-esteem' or 'fear' that would be worth exploring – depending on what other evidence you have gleaned from the client. But we would only recommend introducing those terms to the client if they have used them themselves.

Wait and trust

When you first introduce a client to creativity, it can feel daunting. Mainly this is because you don't know how the client will respond, and it can take a few minutes for them to become engaged in the task. Ensuring that the client has a piece of paper and their creative materials to hand and reassuring them that there is no right or wrong goes a long way to reducing their nerves. Encourage them to listen to their intuition, and if you feel it's helpful, you could bring them to a mindful state, so they are more attuned to their inner self.

Patience is sometimes the key to unlocking the painful wound held within

Sometimes it seems that a client doesn't know how to start and is looking at a blank sheet of paper. In this case, some encouraging words such as, "Trust yourself and your intuition," or, "Just pass your hand over your pens or pencils and see what colour you're drawn to and see what happens," or, "You could try just making marks with your non-dominant hand," and then leave a silent space for them to get underway. Silence is a great enabler and resisting any attempts to intervene with further encouraging words is best. If a client needs to break through their resistance, they need to find their own way to do this. It's about giving the client permission to trust themselves. In our experience, the client soon seems compelled to start and to make something happen.

It is worth noting that a client may find it easier or want to start with a few words. They might look at you and say, "It's like I have a weight on my shoulders," or they might write "weight on my shoulders" or "going round in circles" on their piece of paper. When this happens, ask the client to create "that weight" or "those circles", carefully using their vocabulary. You can further encourage their creative brain to engage by asking, "And that's like what?" If a client writes only words, as sometimes happens, then it may be that an intervention involving storytelling, fairy tales or poetry may be more appropriate. But initially enquiring further about 'circles', or 'weight', with a question such as, "Tell me more about 'circles'," will encourage them to increase their awareness as to what is embedded in the word, and this may be enough for them to create symbols or motifs connected with it.

There is always a learning, a realisation, a discovery to be made that helps the client on their journey

---

We have discovered that something happens once the person picks up a colour that attracts them and starts making marks on the paper. They become absorbed and begin to add details: lines or dots, squiggles, shapes, motifs or words or other materials.

Saying you will remain silent while they work for 5 or 10 minutes gives the client permission to start creating. Setting a fixed, short time lets them know this is a relatively quick exercise. This helps the client to get going and fully engage with their work. However, we encourage the practitioner to let the creative work go on for as long as it seems helpful. This can vary from person to person as most get so absorbed that time seems to fly by.

If the time you have set has elapsed and your client is still working on their creation, you can give them an extra couple of minutes until you can see they are coming naturally to a close. There is no real need to stop them mid-flow. However, some clients, particularly those who are artistic, will often keep going for as long as you give them, so do consider some boundaries! Generally, it's better to have time to explore the image in the same session as the creation work, while there is still a strong connection between the client and their image. It is perfectly okay to return to the image in later sessions, because the client is already familiar with it.

We know of a time when it took six sessions to get past two or three squiggles! These squiggles actually had a story, but the client found it difficult to create any more of the image. Slowly, more and more symbols and metaphors started to emerge, and the client felt compelled to continue to discover more about themselves. Patience is sometimes the key to unlocking the painful wound held within.

When the client has finished

During the creative process, the client can go into a very deep meditative state, but you will know when they have finished because they will generally look up and focus on you again. Quite often, they take a deep breath, rest back in their chair, and are amazed at how engrossed they have been. And amazed by the image in front of them. It is like the image has created itself. Most clients are moved and deeply connected to the image and surprised at what they have experienced.

At this point, the practitioner needs to see their client's creation, so ask the client to hold it up to the camera if you are working online. We recommend asking permission to take a photo of it so you can refer to it; otherwise the client will have to keep holding their image up to the camera, which can become tiring. If you are working face-to-face, it's much easier, and generally you can see more details than online. Whichever way you are viewing the creation, it's key to remember that the questions are directed to the creation, not to the client. You are eliciting what the creation knows, not what the client thinks.

Coming up

In *Step 3*, you will learn how to help the client uncover what the image has to offer. *Step 3* is when the practitioner can pose *The 9 Core Questions* and *Framework Questions* to explore the image as a whole and its component parts, to elicit as much information as possible for the client to reflect upon. We explain how to work with the most simplistic of lines and squiggles to much more complex and involved creations. It is only through this archaeological dig, as we sometimes call it, that a new understanding can emerge.

Summary

The role of the practitioner is to notice when the client seems stuck for words, has a limiting belief, is already using a metaphor or a descriptive phrase to represent their issue, and to decide if creativity would be the most helpful intervention.

Noticing verbal and physical cues is key to finding a topic to work on.

Resist the assumption that you know what metaphors mean.

Metaphors can be such common phrases that the practitioner can miss them unless listening hard for them. This can result in the practitioner rarely stopping to check the meaning.

There is helpful information locked up within the client's words and phrases that they can learn from.

Setting a time limit for the creative task is helpful. 10 minutes is often adequate.

Ensure you have a copy of the image or can clearly see it before moving on to *Step 3: Exploring the Client's Creation*.

Engaging further

View video recordings of our 'Onlinevents' workshops. Use 'creativity' in the search button to find our content and content from other speakers. https://www.courses-onlinevents.co.uk/collections

Book: *The Magic of Metaphor* by Nick Owen

Book: *The Uses of Enchantment: The Meaning and Importance of Fairy Tales* by Bruno Bettelheim

Step 2: The Process of Creation

A question for you

Listen out for verbal metaphors next time you watch TV. What metaphors are often used? What alternative interpretation might there be of them compared to your initial assumption?

5
Step 3: Exploring the Client's Creation

"Don't wait for inspiration.
It comes while working."
Henri Matisse
Painter, draughtsman, printmaker, sculptor

Following the client's lead

As with any counselling or coaching session, we hold as sacred the words our clients introduce and mirror them as closely as we can, even going as far as mirroring the tense the client uses. We do this because each word the client uses has meaning embedded within it, and the practitioner's role is to help them unpack what is going on behind the words.

If a client says, "I am tired of all the noise that is going on inside my head. I just want it to stop," it is important not to try and sanitise it by saying, "Tell me a bit more about the noise that is distracting you." That sentence will have a totally different meaning to the client, and they will start working on something that you introduced, such as 'distracting', rather than what is going on for them. The better way is to ask, "Tell me a bit more about the noise," or, "Tell me about 'going on inside my head'."

Whatever the client says will have a logic that only makes sense to *them*, and if the practitioner shifts the words, even slightly, it can redirect the client, which may lead to a dead-end.

The practitioner must also hold the space for exploration without interpreting the client's creative work

---

To assist the work progressing, care and attention are needed to focus purely on what the client says. This is probably the hardest thing for practitioners to do. As we engage with the client and their image, we can start to think we know how to help the client move to a conclusion by introducing options or suggestions. If we do this, we take power away from the client. A transformation can only happen at the client's pace. The practitioner cannot force this, even if they believe they know what is needed and where to move the client to.

Trusting the client's progress, their vocabulary and journey with their image will pay dividends in helping them achieve the outcome they seek. Over time, as the client changes on the inside, they make mental adjustments to their original beliefs and values, and so too, their image and motifs may change to reflect what is going on for them. For example, when change occurs, a lock that needed a key transforms into a bow that can be undone with a simple tug. Grey foggy mist can become a warm fluffy blanket.

Understanding the Core Questions in more depth

Our presupposition is, and we suggest it is yours too, that everything on or in your client's creation is there for a reason. It has been chosen. It is not random. It has a meaning, a purpose and a message. All the colours (or lack of colours), shapes, textures and materials used will have a role to play in the story, which is the client's unconscious thoughts.

The *Core Questions* we share here are specifically designed to help the client fully explore their image. But nothing can replace your own intuition, and we encourage you to ask whatever questions you feel will help your client the most. As long as you stay engaged with the image, so will your client. That is the magic that will help the client make a transformative shift.

To make magic happen, a practitioner needs to:

- Know *The ChrisLin Method*, but not be a slave to it.
- Remain intensely curious.
- Trust their own intuition to ask the right question at the right time.

Core Question 1: Tell me the story of your image

We say tell me the 'story' of your image because we want to encourage the client to be in storytelling mode. This lays the mental groundwork, the permission if you like, for their intuition to surface and for there to be room for speculation and curiosity. This is very different from a question such as "Tell me what your image means", which presupposes the client already knows what it means. If this is not the case, it can lead to the client mentally shutting down because they don't know what to say or are not ready to share. Or it may lead to them inventing a reply to please you.

Core Question 2: What does this colour represent to you?

As you have already read in *Step 1*, before starting their creative work, the client is guided to be in a state where they can listen more to their intuition rather than their logical brain. And we advise them to 'go with the flow' when it comes to choosing colours. The temptation for anyone in the role of practitioner is to associate colours with meaning from their own frame of reference. For instance, red equals anger, and black must mean a dark feeling. This is dangerous territory! We urge you to be aware of your own assumptions and to suspend them. In our experience, clients can have completely different meanings to the typical way of thinking about colour (if there is such a thing), and the role of the practitioner is to expose the client's interpretation.

The amount of colour used can also vary tremendously. It can range from a simple lead pencil line to an explosion of colour and texture. Take time to explore the colours – whether they are bold, faint, light, dark or smudged – and seek what they represent for the person.

Core Question 3: What does this shape mean for you?

Shapes on the page or in the creation literally come in all shapes and sizes! And in a similar way to colours, the practitioner needs to be careful not to believe they know what the shape is and what it means. Many shapes that appear on our client's images look like something we recognise. Houses, people, flowers, hearts, and tears frequently crop up. But your interpretations may be different from what the person means by them. A house can be a prison; flowers can be a cloud with a centre; tears can be drops of blood. Therefore, we recommend you refer to things as 'shapes'. For instance, "I see there is a shape that appears to be pink and blue. Tell me more about that." Or, "I can see there are some wavy lines in blue. What do they represent?" Only when the client has named the shape can you then use that name.

Sometimes it is impossible to recognise anything because the creation is abstract and a sea of colours and squiggles. However, even with such an image, there will be thicker and thinner lines, or shapes or patterns that overlap or are layered in some way. And each component will have a relationship to the other components on the page. So all of these things are worthy of exploration. For instance, "I notice the image has several colours that overlap one another. Can you tell me more about that?"

If you work with clients several times you may notice that patterns or motifs begin to repeat, albeit with different sizes or colours. Look out for these patterns as they can be critical to the work and may need teasing out. You may say, "I notice that this motif is in several pieces of your work. Can you tell me more about it?" Or a client may notice themselves and say, "Oh, I'm using that motif again."

The number of items can also be significant. "I notice you have a group of three dots there and three straight lines here. Is there anything significant about the number three?" Questions like this can stir memories that have significance to the topic – things like "I have three brothers" or "three friends". And if you just stay with that they may say, "When I was three my mum went into hospital." The unconscious has potentially offered crucial information that the conscious mind needs to hear and make sense of.

Step 3: Exploring the Client's Creation

Core Question 4: What's important about the size of this?

It is rare for an image to have components that are all the same size. Generally, some things will be more significant or feature more strongly than other components, which can be very helpful to explore. Be careful not to assume that because something is small it is of less importance. We remember working with someone who had depicted what looked to us like a tiny rock tucked away in the corner of their image, only to discover that the small 'rock' was a picture of themselves in child pose. This proved to be central to the issue they were dealing with but could so easily have been missed and thought of as insignificant.

Core Question 5: What is in the space(s)?

It is easy to forget about areas that have nothing in them. Our own minds delete this information as being unimportant, so it takes a special effort for the practitioner to notice where there are gaps and spaces. Sometimes you will find that all of the client's work is squashed up into one corner, and the rest of the page is blank, or components are spread across the page not touching one another, or there is one tiny motif on a sheet of A4. It is fascinating what happens when you ask about this emptiness. Clients will have a story for that part too. The unused space has just as rich a story as the image's components, and it is the capacity to notice and the willingness to bring it to the client's attention that is important.

Core Question 6: What is the relationship between this and that?

In almost all images, it is possible to ask a question about the relationship between the components. This is helpful because it is generally not something the client has considered for themselves. For instance, if you noticed a set of squiggles in one part of the image and a set of jagged lines in another, you might ask about the relationship between them. It sounds like an odd question, but it can unravel much new information. One client said, "This represents the part of me that wants to go with the flow, and this part represents the part that wants to fight back. They are battling one another the whole time." The practitioner and the client now know there are two parts to the client's thinking, and they are in conflict. Another client said, "I have a lot of energy here, but this is a boundary that I can't cross, and it's stopping me." Whatever the image offers, it will add to the knowledge of the client and the practitioner.

Core Question 7: If this image had a voice, what would it say?

This is a very powerful question because it enables the unconscious to have a voice. At last, the unconscious gets a chance to speak about its beliefs, wants and needs, and further questioning along these lines is always fruitful. By bringing the unconscious into the conscious mind, the client can hear it for the first time. And with this new-found knowledge, they can start to understand and evaluate the purpose of the unconscious and what it is trying to do.

Brave voices can speak the truth without editing

Core Question 8: What does the image know now that it didn't know before?

It is essential to grasp the language of this question. By asking the question in the way we suggest, we presuppose there is knowledge to be uncovered, and it encourages the client to find answers and new meanings. It is a softer way to help them notice any movement in their understanding and is much more effective than asking "What do you know now?" (which moves the client away from the image) or "What have you learnt?" (which makes it feel like a test and also draws the client away from listening to the creation).

Core Question 9: Is there anything else you need to add or take away from the image to represent the change that has happened?

At this stage, it's helpful to ask the client to review their image and ask them if they want to make any changes to represent their new understanding or feeling. Again, we work from the presupposition that something has happened and that something will have changed that will impact the original image. When given this opportunity, many clients say, "Oh, I'd definitely take this off," or, "I'd make this bigger," or, "I think I need to add…." You can encourage people to make the change there and then by asking, "And can you make that change?" followed by, "And will you make that change now?" There is a subtle difference in the outcome of these two questions – the first will elicit the desire or intent to make the change, and the second will test the willingness to make the change.

For example, some people will say they can make the change but are unwilling to do so now, indicating something unresolved. It may be worth exploring what is getting in their way. Others might say they can't make the change because, for instance, they don't have the materials or time, but they are willing to do so. If the client can and is ready to make the change, we suggest giving them a few minutes to do so in whatever way they choose. When they have finished, you will immediately see that they are much happier with the image and feel proud of it!

It is important to note that there may be a component, or components, of the image that the client no longer feels belong there. In some instances, it is possible to work with this, and we recommend that you do, as there is important information in everything the client has created. Rather than the client just taking it off and throwing it away, it may be more appropriate to investigate this piece separately to help it have its say and the opportunity to be accepted or gain permission to transform. It can be helpful to ask if the client wants to recreate this component on a separate piece of paper or in another medium so that it can be looked at in its own right to discover more about it and what needs to happen next.

Alternatively, the client may need to find a way to let this component go – carefully, respectfully and compassionately – or consider if forgiveness is necessary.

Coming up

We work on the principle that if you take something 'out' of the client, as you do when you ask someone to create something outside of themselves, it is good to put something 'back'. By now, the client has gained a new understanding of themselves and perhaps made changes to their image to reflect their new-found knowledge. Now it is time to integrate the learning back into themselves, and in Chapter 6 we discuss integration and a variety of ways to embody the change, which is the road to long-lasting impact.

Summary

The *9 Core Questions* can be used in any creative session and if followed will produce a good outcome.

The biggest challenge for practitioners is to refrain from interpreting or making assumptions about the image and the components in the client's creative piece.

The practitioner's role is to know *The ChrisLin Method* but not be a slave to it.

Remain intensely curious and trust your intuition to ask the right question.

When the client has finished exploring their image and making any changes, the practitioner moves to *Step 4* to embody the change and *Step 5* to close the session.

Engaging further

Book: *Working With Images: The Art of Art Therapists* by Bruce L Moon

Book: *The Artist's Way* by Julia Cameron

A question for you

Having been through all the *Core Questions*, which ones are you drawn to and why?

6

Step 4: Integrating the Changes

"Most people do not listen with the intent to understand; they listen with the intent to reply."
Stephen R Covey
*Author, educator, businessman
and keynote speaker*

Putting something back

We work on the principle that if you take something 'out' of the client, as you do when you ask someone to create something outside of themselves, it is good to put something 'back'.

In almost all circumstances the practitioner will see a physical change in the client as a result of the creative process. The client will look calmer, softer, be smiling and seem lighter and brighter to some degree, depending on their journey. This physical change is another of those moments that can pass by the client and the practitioner in an instant, and the importance is lost if you're not careful. Integration is about capturing that moment and embodying the change, so the client acknowledges the change that has taken place in their body and has a sense of it becoming part of them and of welcoming it home.

How integration happens depends on several things, not least what the client wants to do. The client, after all, is in charge. But many clients are happy to be led by the practitioner in a small ritual to embody the learning. It can be as simple as suggesting the client holds their image to their heart and 'breathes it in' with a deep inhale. For some clients, this is all they need to recognise, that they feel physically different and that mentally they have more choices about how to respond to the topic they have been working on. They will often say, "Wow, that looks and feels so different. It's hard to understand how my image has had so much impact."

The ChrisLin Method brings the unconscious drivers and hidden knowledge to the conscious mind

---

You may have your own way of integrating and embodying change. For instance, using mindfulness to connect the client's mind and body and focus on the change that has occurred. Alternatively, they could use visualisation to create a solid mental picture of themselves and the attributes and qualities they have gathered from the work they have done. Or by taking time to look into the future and how things will be different. Or using breathwork to help the client become grounded and receptive to let the change in.

Bringing the new behaviour to mind, thinking and imagining themselves acting differently during the embodiment can trigger a body simulation of the experience and help encode and integrate the new way of being. Many practices, such as the ones listed below, can support the healing process, increasing self-awareness and self-acceptance and connecting the mind, body and spirit.

Embodiment and integration techniques

- Holding the image to the heart and breathing it in
- Visualisation
- Dance or body movement
- Mindfulness
- Meditation
- Yoga
- Interoception – awareness skills for emotional regulation
- Breathwork
- Grounding techniques
- Sensory engagement – walking barefoot, listening to nature, forest bathing
- Muscle relaxation techniques or stretching

However, some clients are happy to skip the embodiment and go straight to the final stage, *Step 5*, deciding what to do with their image, which we cover in Chapter 7.

Maintaining the change

As mentioned above, integration takes many forms, and the change can sometimes take a little while to settle into the person. The client who takes a deep breath and sees and feels things differently straight away may be someone who is fully engaged with their intuition and feelings and can adopt the change quickly. Someone else may need to go back into the real world and test out the changes to be entirely sure that something has happened before their logical brain can accept it. It may take a while for these clients to adapt to the change and allow it to stick around and help carry them forward.

Regular reminders to mentally visualise the present or step into the future, to experience the changes and how they are going to act differently, can reinforce and embed the knowledge that a change has occurred.

> *"I would never have imagined I could do that. It has always been so hard. But now I can feel the difference and realise I do have the ability to do things differently."*
> **Julie, client, Perth, Australia**

Coming up

In the next chapter, we describe how to bring the session to a close and take the opportunity to check in with the client regarding their original goal or outcome. We recommend that the practitioner leads a discussion about the creative piece to establish what the client wants to do with it and provides some ideas and options to do so safely and compassionately.

Summary

We work on the principle that if you take something 'out' of the client, as you do when you ask someone to create something outside of themselves, it is good to put something 'back'.

The physical and mental changes the client experiences when concluding a creative session are important and need to be captured.

Integration is about embodying the change so the client embeds the new way of being.

Embodiment, or integrative practices, can increase self-awareness and self-acceptance and connect the mind, body and spirit.

Repetition can further reinforce the change.

Engaging further

Book: *The Body Keeps the Score* by Bessel van der Kolk

Book: *The Art of Somatic Coaching: Embodying Skillful Action, Wisdom, and Compassion* by Richard Strozzi-Heckler

Book: *Awakening the Heroes Within: Twelve Archetypes to Help Us Find Ourselves and Transform Our World* by Carol S Pearson

A question for you

What technique to help clients integrate and embody their experience are you drawn to? What else might you need to learn to help the client embody change?

7
Step 5: Closing the Session

"If you don't like something, change it. If you can't change it, change your attitude."
Maya Angelou
Author, poet and civil rights activist

Has the desired outcome been satisfied?

Before ending the session, it's helpful to review if the client's original desired outcome, if there was one, has been satisfied. However, it is common for the issue and/or outcome to have changed significantly during the process. This is because the client may have moved from wanting to get away from, or stop, or not have or not do, into a resourced state where an outcome is now possible – of being in control, starting, having, saying and acting in a way that positively supports them. They have moved from unhelpful emotions and behaviours to helpful ones.

What to do with the creation

Finishing a session with the question "What would you like to do with your creation next?" is an excellent segue into a discussion about what the client wants to do with their image.

Clients vary significantly in this regard. Some have a very clear idea of where they will put it, such as on a shelf or wall where they can see it. Others want to keep it, but out of sight, like in a drawer, and some want to crunch it up and put it in the bin because the work is done! Like so much of this work, there is no right or wrong. It's more about going with the flow and supporting the client to do what seems right to them.

It is also possible for the client to ask the practitioner to keep it safe in case they want to work on it again or just because it feels complete and they want to leave it in safe hands. In this case, it is probably wise to keep the image until after the work with the client is fully finished, as they may ask, several sessions later, to view it again! It's also prudent to tell them that you have a policy of only holding a client's information for a set period of time, so they know you will not be holding it indefinitely.

Symbolic endings

For some topics, when the client is already thinking about letting go of something they find unhelpful or challenging to deal with, we suggest an alternative way of symbolising an ending. However, this technique can be used for many situations where the client needs to leave a thought or emotion behind. It involves creating a ritual, engaging one of the four elements – earth, air, fire or water – to assist in the letting go and honouring its passing. The elements can translate into (environmentally sound and responsible) actions such as burning the image, imagining blowing it off into the wind, floating it down a river or burying it in the earth.

Step 5: Closing the Session

Whatever method is selected, it brings a sense of closure, having dealt with something and moved it away from unhelpfully influencing the present and future, which is immensely healing.

Coming up

Through years of testing and refining *The ChrisLin Method* with clients and fellow practitioners, we have discovered that our process is very robust and enables significant shifts to take place quickly and easily. And we know that if you have the confidence to trust the process, you will bring about changes that release your clients from their burdens and help to positively shape their lives. From session to session this change may be small or a transformational one, but either way you will be supporting your client and enabling them to become better resourced, be more in control of their lives and feel a greater sense of self-worth.

In the following chapters, you will find an example of a client session using only *The 9 Core Questions* so you can see them in action, followed by three *Frameworks* – for working with anxiety, boundaries and anger. Each *Framework* includes a unique creative approach and set of questions specifically developed to assist with the exploration of the topic. They also include a case study that demonstrates the use of *The 9 Core Questions* alongside the specific *Framework Questions*.

And finally, we hope you will see how transformative *The ChrisLin Method* is and how it deserves to be a valuable addition to your toolkit.

"Every valuable creative idea must always be logical in hindsight. If it were not, we would never be able to see its value."
Edward de Bono – *Author, psychologist and physiologist*

Summary

Before ending the session, it is helpful to review the client's original desired outcome to see if it has been satisfied and check they have moved from unhelpful emotions and behaviours to helpful ones.

It is good practice to give the client the opportunity to find a home for their creative piece, even if that home is floating off down a physical or metaphorical river.

When letting go of an unhelpful emotion or behaviour, the client can enlist one of the four elements to create a ritual to honour its passing.

Engaging further

Book: *Cutting the Ties That Bind: Growing Up and Moving On* by Phyllis Krystal

Book: *Stop the Excuses! How to Change Lifelong Thoughts* by Dr Wayne Dyer

A question for you

Now that you have finished this section of the book, which chapters do you want to keep a note of because you'll want to go back to them in the future, and which sections might you need to read again?

8
Case Study Using The 9 Core Questions

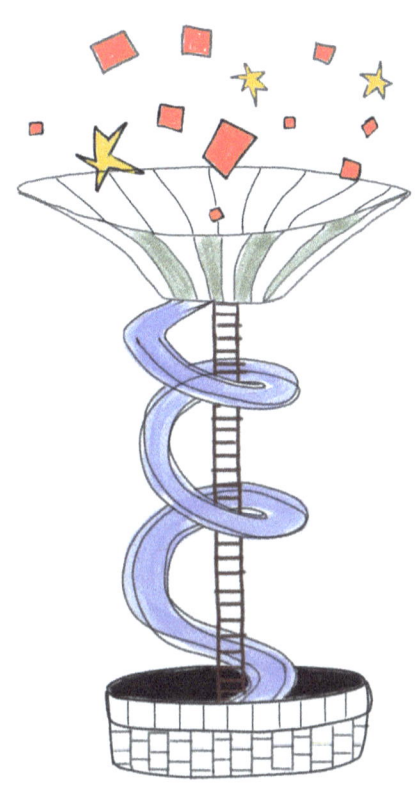

Introduction to the case study

Having familiarised yourself with our theories and experiences of working creatively, we would like to help you become even more confident to work creatively with your clients.

Below, we share a case study to demonstrate *Step 3: Exploring the Client's Creation*. We can assume that *Step 1* and *Step 2* have already taken place and that the practitioner is now ready to help the client explore their creation using *The 9 Core Questions*.

This case study showcases the practical application of the *Core Questions* in a session and highlights how they facilitate a gentle but powerful journey of discovery.

Each question is referenced as CQ1 for *Core Question* 1, CQ2 for *Core Question* 2, and so on.

Case Study

Background

Thomas is trying to make his mind up about something that will impact his life going forward. He is finding it hard to make a decision about where to live. He has spent several years going round and round in circles and has been unable to commit fully to moving or staying where he is. His friends have become fed up with hearing the same story and just want him to decide. He is very frustrated with himself as he believes he wants to come to some conclusion but can't understand what is getting in his way. He says he is just "going round and round in circles".

What would you like to get from the session today?

"I just want to make a decision and move on with my life. That means deciding whether I stay here or move."

Factors influencing the issue

Thomas is someone who has made many spontaneous decisions in his life, but he has not been able to do that with this particular decision. He generally doesn't put a lot of thought into decisions to do with himself and has spent a lifetime taking risks, assuming it will all turn out okay in the end. He recognises that this has led to some outcomes that were not in his best interests and have contributed to his current situation. He always thought he would move back to the seaside and live out his life walking the coastal paths and enjoying making new friends and starting new hobbies. However, as life has progressed and he has established a life where he is now, he feels he may have left it too late to start again. This is not helped by friends who fall into two camps: some who say "Just do it" and others who say "Stay where you are." The other factor is that he believes downsizing would help release some money to supplement his income.

Exploring the client's creative work

It was suggested to Thomas that he create an image to represent his issue and where he is now with it. He was asked: "When going round and round in circles, that's like what?" He replied that it was like a spiral staircase that sucks him down to the bottom and he gets tangled up at the bottom for a while before he can escape and come back up. But then the cycle starts again.

Thomas was invited to create a representation of his issue, and he drew a spiral that took up the length of the page. It had a second spiral to one side and several squares and two jagged red shapes at the top of the page, and various squiggles and lines. The entrance to the spiral looked like a funnel.

CQ1: Tell me the story of your image

"Well, it looks like a spiral, but the action is circular. I go down to the bottom of the spiral, and then I get stuck. And then I come up to the top, and I get stuck. And I go down to the bottom, and I get stuck. So that's what it feels like. It feels like it's something deep that I get into. So I go round in circles and up and down the spiral. Even saying that makes me feel confused."

Thomas spent a few moments looking at his image.

"When I'm at the top of the spiral, I start noticing all the things that I've got. And when I get down to the bottom, I sort of see all the things that I haven't got yet, but could, if I get on with sorting out this move. I've drawn this as a spiral shape, but it's really a slide because once I'm on it, there is no stopping. It's like a helter-skelter. I end up in this deep well, which has got a box around it. So in a funny sort of way, it's quite safe when I'm there. Then at the top of the image, I've got things like bright sunshine; again this feels safe. So when I'm at the top or at the bottom, all is well. It is the journey up and down the spiral where I feel out of control."

CQ2: What does this colour represent to you?

"Those red star shapes I think are me. I'm waiting at the top of the spiral. I can stay there for a while, and then it feels like I lose control and drop down the slide into the well at the bottom."

CQ3: What do these shapes mean for you?

"Those boxes are the compartments of my life that I have now. One box represents work, one my family and one represents my home and all the things I am familiar with. They are the things that are important to me, but somehow, they also feel stuck. As I look at it, there are three places I feel stuck. There is the entrance to the spiral, there is the well at the bottom, and the boxes. That's a lot of stuckness that I hadn't realised before! It's not as simple as I thought. And there's that second spiral off to one side, more like a labyrinth thing."

As Thomas starts to investigate his image, he gains some clarity. He is beginning to look at the process he is going through and identifying complexities he hadn't previously known anything about. It seemed it might be helpful to explore the second spiral that Thomas called 'labyrinth' by using CQ3 question again.

CQ3: What does this shape mean for you? (Pointing to the labyrinth.)

"Well, that is a labyrinth. I don't really understand it, but it is there."

Thomas was left to ponder on his labyrinth.

"Sometimes when I go down the slide, I get side-tracked and enter the labyrinth. I start thinking about myself and how I've messed things up and feeling sorry for myself. To make myself feel better I start doing a bit of research or start making plans to get rid of things because that feels like it's some action and the right thing to do. But the labyrinth has a deep well, just like the well at the bottom of the slide. It's very odd because there's something very familiar about the entrance at the top of the spiral and the bottom of the spiral and getting trapped in the labyrinth."

Thomas went very still and quiet for several minutes. He was processing something that needed time.

"When I was young, we were given a lot of freedom to make choices and I made the choice to leave school at 16. As I think of that now, I just wanted my father to tell me that I had to go to school. But once I'd made that decision, I could not go back on my own accord, and he took no responsibility to get me engaged in education again. That spiral at the side seems to represent that same problem. A need for someone, him, to tell me what to do. That's what I think I've been waiting for. Someone else to make the decision. None of it feels safe but it all feels familiar. I now feel both angry with my dad and sad that it has taken me so long to discover this."

Notice how Thomas has started to understand all the connected parts of the strategy he is currently operating, and he has begun to understand the root of what is happening. This seems to be a turning point for him, and he needs to process it further. This processing can happen in his unconscious while other things are explored.

CQ4: What's important about the size of the boxes?

"What's important about the size of the boxes? Well, interestingly enough, they feel very small. And what I think is safe is not really safe because, at any moment in time, they can disappear. My friends can choose to pack up and move, and my work can suddenly stop. So although they feel safe at first glance, they only feel safe at this moment in time. Looking at them now, they feel very unsafe and unstable. That's quite an eye-opener. I'm realising my life is pretty unstable, yet it's what I have relied on."

CQ5: What is in the space between the boxes and the spiral?

"Well, as I look at it, the space is a waiting space and, in that space, those red parts that are me are floating about. They are waiting. And then they get close to the funnel, and it sucks them in. It's a bit like a distraction mechanism. They get pushed to decide but don't know which way to turn so they hang about in the space. There needs to be a barrier at the top of the funnel to stop them from being sucked in. I want to create a barrier – so it's much harder to get into the funnel."

Thomas creates a fence around the top of the funnel so there is no easy way in.

"The red shapes feel like they are in conflict with each other: one wants to move to the seaside and the other wants to stay locally. But both want to move, they just don't know where to. Oh! That's it! So the decision is actually about *where* to go and not about staying or going. Well, that's quite an insight!"

CQ6: What is the relationship between the spiral and the labyrinth?

"What is weird, now that I have put the fence along the top of the funnel, it all looks really different. The spiral is no longer looking like something that traps me and I can see an easy way out of the labyrinth. I'm not quite sure how the fence has changed what I'm seeing now.

The whole picture looks more fluid. It feels like everything has slowed down and there are choices. However, what I'm also realising is that the things I have up to now thought of as certain, are not. That's not really bothered me before, but for this decision, it really seems important to do it for the right reasons and make it a good decision. So, there's something about taking charge of my situation, and actually, if I'm honest, it's like taking real responsibility. Funnily enough, just acknowledging that makes me feel more at peace and more certain."

Thomas took a breath and brought his hand to his forehead like he was wiping away sweat.

CQ7: If this image had a voice, what would it say?

"It's time for you now to say, 'Right, own the decision. Think about the consequences for each option and then just do it,' in a really commanding voice that I need to obey."

CQ8: What does the image know now that it didn't know before?

"Well, what suddenly comes into my head is that you have to do it for yourself, don't you? It feels like I've been waiting for someone or something else to make the decision. I know now that it's down to me, and I need to stop wasting energy thinking about it and take action. It feels like the first grown-up decision I've ever made. It has to come from me, by myself, alone – I have to make the choice."

Thomas sighed and briefly looked away.

"I've known that all along but have been in denial. Now it's there right in front of me and can't be denied."

CQ9: Is there anything you need to add or take away from the image to represent the change that has happened?

"Now that I really look at the image, I'm seeing different things and I think what the image needs is a ladder from the well to the top. I now see that the well holds a lot of information that I've collected so far, and I may want to visit it from time to time."

Thomas looked at his creation for a short while then picked up three different coloured felt tip pens and started to draw a ladder right up through the spiral. He blocked off the link to the side spiral and sat back and took a deep breath.

"Oh my god, I can see my life opening out in front of me, with a whole new pathway. I'm not sure how that happened, but all the knots I had in my stomach at the start of this have disappeared. I didn't even know how tense all this has been making me until the tension has gone."

Step 4: Integrating the changes: What needs to happen next?

"This ladder means I can go up and down under my own control and I can check that I am only taking useful information with me. I don't have to slide down and I don't have to go off at a tangent and feel sorry for myself. I can be an adult now who is able to make adult decisions that are in my best interests. It's about time! What I now need is a plan and a goal. Let's see; by the next bank holiday I want to be ready to put my house on the market."

Thomas was invited to look at his image and imagine stepping out into the future to the next bank holiday and then, in his mind's eye, turn around and look back to today and notice all the steps he had taken to achieve his plan. He was able to see the immediate steps he needed to take, such as clearing and repairing his house, researching where to look for a new home and which estate agent to use.

Step 5: Closing the session: What do you want to do with your image?

"I think I'm going to keep it in the short term to remind me of my plan and that I have choices. But I think after a few weeks I'll throw it away. I don't need to keep it. I think I've learnt what I needed to learn."

9
Introducing the ChrisLin Frameworks

How to use the Frameworks

The *Frameworks* we provide here are creative methods designed specifically for working with certain emotions, behaviours or models. For example, in Chapters 10-12, we provide *Frameworks* for working with anxiety, boundaries and anger, which we commonly see in the therapy room.

The *Frameworks* include a discussion on the topic, an explanation of our approach and what we think is generally at the root of the issue, so you are aware of where the matter might go. We also offer helpful hints about what to look and listen for when clients share their thoughts.

Within each *Framework* is:

- A step-by-step guide to the unique creative method.
- Specific *Framework Questions* designed to help the client dig a little deeper into the topic. These *Framework Questions* are used in conjunction with *The 9 Core Questions*, which, together, provide a rich exploratory experience.
- A case study to demonstrate the application of the creative method in a real-life situation so you observe the principles of the method and become familiar with the process.

How do you know when to use a *Framework* for a specific emotion or behaviour?

Mostly this is by listening to the language of your client. For example, we use the *Anxiety Framework* if the client says things like, "I'm feeling very anxious a lot of the time," or, "I'm really getting worried about leaving the house." Our clients tell us what they need to work on when we listen. And you do this all the time, so, trust your instincts to use a *Framework* as part of your professional toolkit.

Once you become familiar with the creative methods in all the *Frameworks*, you will be able to select which one to use based on your understanding of your client's needs and use them interchangeably to great effect.

The case studies – things to consider

- The case studies show the overall flow, and some of the key questions – not all of them – that helped move the client towards further clarity or resolution of their issue.
- We demonstrate the use of the *Steps, Core Questions* and *Framework Questions* so you can see how they work together.
- We role model staying focused on the client's image and ensuring the client is telling the image's story, so they benefit from this deeper knowledge.
- Several sessions are often needed for all the information to surface and be worked with.

We hope you will get to know and love working creatively as much as we do and gain satisfaction from the difference it makes to your clients.

10
Framework for Working with Anxiety: Separating Imagination from Reality

What is anxiety?

We all experience anxiety in our lives, from worrying about our kids or parents, making a presentation and financial concerns to worrying about relationships or broader issues with uncertain outcomes. Anxiety, in this regard, is a normal part of the human condition and can be helpful in moderation. It helps us think ahead, prepare and consider risks.

But more often than not, our client's anxiety presents as being unhelpful and sometimes debilitating. Clients say their thoughts are out of control, they can no longer function, their brain is foggy, or they feel overwhelmed and exhausted with the constant churn. This sort of anxiety can be hard to change, rooted as it is in a well-used pattern of thought and often deeply entrenched.

It is generally accepted that fear and anxiety generate the same or very similar responses. Clients often report feeling sweaty, their heart beating faster and breathing more heavily, which are typical fear responses. Experiencing this over an extended period of time seems to drain energy and the capacity to think clearly, and this can spiral out of control.

Many practitioners will be familiar with the fight or flight response. However, anxiety and fear are different. Research indicates that a fear response results from a "known *external* danger", and anxiety can be a reaction to a *perceived* threat, or a "generalised response to an unknown threat or internal conflict". Both create brain and bodily alarms to alert us to danger. But in many cases of anxiety, the alarm is stuck 'on', and people seem to be perpetually in alert mode, constantly scanning for threats.

Understanding this about anxiety was key to developing the *Framework* we discuss here. It helps clients understand what is happening to them so they can separate predictions, assumptions and imagination from what is real and recognise when the imagination is taking control. When a client works on one of their anxieties, they experience how to change their thought pattern and reduce the impact of the fear response in their body. With the help of the practitioner or even alone, they can apply the *Framework* to other anxieties to help train themselves to learn a different way of dealing with perceived threats.

Our approach

We call anxiety an emotion of the future. Often when clients are anxious, they imagine a time in the future when something might happen, but they have no evidence that it definitely will happen, such as not getting a job, failing exams, missing an appointment or the outcome of some health issue for themselves or someone else. These predictions feel real and so create the physical symptoms that people experience. Helping clients to disentangle the imagined future from what is real is often enough to create space to breathe and change a client's mindset.

We all tell ourselves a lot of stories, but people vary in what they consider a cause of anxiety. What one person feels anxious about, such as a fear of going to a party, someone else may be quite relaxed about. Some people may be generally anxious all the time, while others worry about specific situations or issues. Nevertheless, clients express common effects, such as an inability to make decisions, lack of concentration and motivation, head in a whirl, insomnia, and mental and physical exhaustion, regardless of the cause of their anxiousness.

Clients' predictions can be based on what has happened in the past. Someone might say, "Well, last time I went to a party I had a panic attack, and it was just awful." The assumption is that because it happened last time, it must be true that it will happen in the future. In some respects, this fits with the purpose of anxiety; after all, being able to analyse risk and predict problems is a helpful human ability. But when the alarm is constantly stuck 'on', the brain sees everything as a challenge and is stuck in a loop. Our *Framework* helps to break that loop and enable a different way of thinking.

What do we think is generally the root cause of anxiety?

It is often difficult for clients to label this emotion as anything other than anxiety, but in our experience, when clients dig a little deeper, the root of the anxiety is often something like anger, shame, fear or grief, but it can also be other emotions. Using the *Anxiety Framework* provides an opportunity for the client to first untangle their thoughts and secondly identify the drivers behind their anxious behaviour.

How might anxiety show up?

There are too many variations to write here, but some of the more common themes are listed below, and we are sure you will recognise many of them in your clients and perhaps yourself. Clients frequently talk about their physical symptoms, and they also say, "I am a really anxious person. I worry about everything." When you get them to write down the things they are worrying about, the list can become quite long, from forgetting something minor to predicting that they will suffer a life-limiting illness in the future.

Anxiety topics

- Social – concerns about being in groups, travelling, planning, having nothing to say, being liked
- External conflict – relationship problems, problems with work colleagues, neighbours
- Internal conflict – beliefs, culture, religion, secrets, acceptance, belonging, love
- Finances – unemployment, unexpected costs, debt
- Friends and family – worry about another individual
- Health – concerns about their own or other people's health, losing someone
- Work stress – presentations, expectations, workload, speaking up, promotion, job security
- Environment and world conflict

In this chapter's case study, we provide an example of working with a client. It is important to recognise that this is a snapshot of the process and not a verbatim account of the whole session. We have endeavoured to select moments where change has taken place to illustrate the flow and use of the *Core Questions* and *Framework Questions* in a real situation.

Engaging further

Book: *The Anxiety Workbook: Practical Tips and Guided Exercises to Help You Overcome Anxiety* by Anna Barnes

Book: *Thinking Like Magic: Transform your Mental Wellbeing* by Karen Kimberley

Anxiety Framework
Creative Process

1. Identify the anxiety the client wants to work on.
2. Invite the client to write down all their predictions and assumptions and what they are imagining will happen. This is called 'Predictions'.
3. Invite the client to write down what they know to be real and true, *right now, in this moment*. This is called 'Reality'.
4. Looking at the list called Reality, ask the client to create a representation of reality using their creative materials.
5. Explore reality using a selection of questions from *The 9 Core Questions* and the following *Framework Questions*:
    a. What does reality know now about the written Predictions?
    b. What is Reality responsible for?
    c. Is there anything Reality needs to say, think or do?
6. Having heard what Reality has had to say, give the list called Predictions a voice by exploring what it knows now, using the following *Framework Questions*:
    d. What does your written Prediction know now that it didn't know before?
    e. Is there anything Predictions needs to say, think or do?
7. Explore what the client has learnt from listening to Predictions and Reality that will help them develop a strategy for managing anxiety in the future, using the following *Framework Questions*:
    f. What have you learnt about your specific anxiety today?
    g. What can you take forward that will help you in the future?

As a reminder, it's not necessary to ask all of the questions on every occasion. The case study below demonstrates how we have selected questions from *The Core Questions* and the above list of *Framework Questions* to help the client understand more about themselves and their issue and make a positive shift. As you become familiar with *The ChrisLin Method* you will be able to confidently select questions on the fly as well as adding questions of your own, based on your own intuition.

Introduction to the case study

In this case study we demonstrate how to select questions from *The 9 Core Questions* and the *Framework Questions* so you can see how they work together. We reference the questions as CQ1 for *Core Question* 1, CQ2 for *Core Question* 2, and so on, and FQa, FQb, and so on for questions from the *Framework*.

The specific *Framework Questions* for this topic are:

a. What does reality know now about the written Predictions?

b. What is Reality responsible for?

c. Is there anything Reality needs to say, think or do?

d. What does your written Prediction know now that it didn't know before?

e. Is there anything Predictions needs to say, think or do?

f. What have you learnt about your specific anxiety today?

g. What can you take forward that will help you in the future?

Case Study

Background

Lena's mindset in life was to focus on what could go wrong. Her life was shrouded in one difficulty after another, and she focused largely on what people thought or felt about her. Things such as the bus being late or no parking spaces confirmed that nothing went right for her, and she would say, "I knew that would happen." Lena's main focus was her concern about her mental wellbeing and how her anxiety was controlling her life.

What would you like to get from the session today?

"I want to feel positive and change my mindset, so I am focusing on brighter things."

Factors influencing the issue

Lena was an only child growing up, and she remembered her parents always being worried about something. Did they have enough money to keep the family in their desired lifestyle? What would the neighbours think if she misbehaved, or if her dad lost his job? It was imperative that people had a good opinion of them as a family. On top of this, there was a family secret. Her mum and dad had different religions, and this had caused a family scandal, so had to be kept quiet. Punishment was harsh if Lena stepped out of line, so she spent her life monitoring what she said and did. She tried to manage what she felt – because she believed that fitting in was crucial for being loved.

Exploring the client's creative work

The first step of this *Framework* is to ask the client to create a list of their predictions about their issue.

Lena was asked to write a list of predictions and assumptions about something she was really anxious about and that she thought about regularly. This was to be the focus of the work for this session. Lena said she was constantly worried about her mental wellbeing and its effect on her and her family.

Her list of predictions and assumptions included things like:

- I worry that I'm going mad.
- People think I'm weak.
- I'm not a good role model for my kids because I'm always stressed.
- People think I'm a useless mother.
- I might have a nervous breakdown and be hospitalised and then what would happen to the kids?
- People at work think I don't pull my weight. They deliberately make my life difficult.
- I never have any luck.
- I will get a terminal illness.
- I don't follow a religion, and I probably should. I'll probably go to hell.

The second step of the *Framework* is to ask the client to write a list of what is real and true, *right at this moment*. It is helpful to settle or ground the client so they can focus on the here and now, which can be done with a grounding or mindfulness technique or simply some examples such as "I am sat on a chair and my back is supported" or "I'm dry and warm here even though it's raining outside" or "I can hear cars on the road outside and the birds singing" or "Right now I have enough food in the house to make dinner tonight". She was guided to write only what was true at this moment and resist providing caveats such as "I don't have a cold at the moment, but I pick up infections easily". She wrote:

- Today I am okay.
- I feel anxious, but I am not having a panic attack.
- I have taken my tablets for my anxiety, so I feel pretty calm.
- I'm not going mad today!
- I have a small issue with my ankle, and it's a bit swollen.
- I don't have a terminal illness.
- I meditated this morning, which made me feel a bit calmer.
- I feel safe in my home.
- I have enough food in the fridge to make lunch and dinner for the kids and us.
- My kids are at school.
- My husband got off to work today okay.
- I can hear the birds in the garden and the traffic on my road.

Lena was asked to look at her list of reality, things that she knew to be true, and create an image that summed up and represented 'reality'. Lena was given 5 minutes to complete her image.

Lena's image was an outline of a person looking strong and well balanced with a large heart shape in the middle. It had a head of curly hair and bright eyes, and inside was a small image of a person lying down and sleeping with a few z's and some other symbols.

CQ1: Tell me the story of your image

"I'm trying to show someone who is really strong and healthy and feels calm in their head. I have moments when I feel just like this."

CQ3: What does that shape inside the head mean for you?

"It's a person lying down listening to music. I don't quite know why I drew a body lying down, but listening to music takes me to another place. And in that image, she is in a very peaceful and spiritual place. I've forgotten how important music used to be to me."

CQ6: What is the relationship between these lines at the bottom and what is going on inside the head?

"The lines at the bottom are the ground. It's kind of firm and solid. The person is standing on it. The happy music can play in the head when it's like that. But when I'm anxious, it's like that ground shakes, and the legs go to jelly, and the whole body shakes. That's when I can't think straight."

Lena paused and studied the image.

"I didn't know that. That's exactly what it feels like."

Notice Lena is able to use the metaphor to notice and describe what happens when she becomes anxious in a way that she may not have been able to before.

FQb: What is Reality responsible for?

"What's it responsible for? Umm. Keeping her grounded and in the moment. Reality needs to keep reminding her to focus on what she knows right now in this moment, as that is really solid, and the anxiety has no room there."

CQ7: If your Reality image had a voice, what would it say?

"Stay close to me, listen to me, and you will stay calm and safe."

Lena was invited to bring her written predictions close to her image of reality.

FQd: What do your written Predictions know now that they did not know before?

Lena looked thoughtful and pondered on this for a few moments.

"All these things could happen, but they also may not."

FQe: Is there anything Predictions needs to say, think or do?

"Yes, they thought they were getting her to pay attention to stuff and keep her from doing things that might become a problem. They were saying all the things that *could* be a problem. It's like the predictions were finding every single thing that could possibly go wrong."

Lena was asked the same question again to see if it would move her on.

FQe: Is there anything Predictions needs to say, think or do?

"Well, in terms of what they need to think or do, they need to stop thinking everything is a risk and do something different! That unless they have something meaningful and useful to add then they have no need to speak out. Just looking at the list now just makes me feel overwhelmed. But, if I look at each one, I can see that I'm letting my imagination run away with me. Half of those things are just not true anyway! Maybe the predictions should just shut up for a while and figure out how to only tell me when something is really important."

FQf: What have you learnt about your specific anxiety today?

"That I need to think a bit harder about things that I feel anxious about and question them some more. I think I had just accepted that all the worry and concern was the only way to live. I didn't know I had a choice about it. I already feel calmer. I can make up my own mind. It's as if my body has let go of something it didn't need."

FQg: What can you take forward that will help you in the future?

"I really like my strong image. I want to keep that as a reminder. I need a mantra! 'What do I know to be real and true right now, in this moment?' And I'd like to think about how I can listen to music more. I had forgotten how important music used to be to me. That is such a relief. I feel so much better!"

CQ9: Is there anything you need to add or take away from the image to represent the change that has happened?

"Yes, I'd really like to add my mantra and a reminder to listen to music regularly."

Lena was invited to make that change now and given a few moments to do so.

Lena has reached a good point in this session, and it seemed to be a good time to lead her into Step 4 – Integration, to embody the change.

The next question reflects back on what she wanted to achieve in the session today.

Step 4: Looking forward into the future, do you feel positive, and can you focus on brighter things?

"I believe so. I feel quite different. I'm thinking about some music right now and I already feel stronger and ready to move forward. I will keep that image close by and connect with it until this becomes my new reality."

Lena was invited to add the music to her image and given a few moments to do so.

To integrate the change, Lena was led through an exercise that involved breathwork and visualisation. She was asked to pick up her image, hold it to her chest, close her eyes and imagine herself feeling positive and brighter and reminded that she had choices and felt stronger and ready to move forward. She was asked to breathe it all in. She was then asked to imagine stepping forward to tomorrow, asking herself, "What do I know to be real and true right now, in this moment." She was asked to visualise herself allowing all these things to flow through her body, taking all the time she needed to feel what she felt, all the way out to the tips of her fingers and to the tips of her toes. Looking into the future and noticing what choices she now had and the change that had taken place.

As Lena connected with her image, her face softened, and her breathing became rhythmic as her body relaxed. After a few moments Lena was asked to come back to the present. She said she felt relaxed and that it was a completely new feeling for her.

To close the session Lena was asked what she wanted to do with her image.

Step 5: As we end the session today, I wonder what you would like to do with your image.

"That's a no-brainer: I'm going to take a photo of it and have it as the wallpaper on my phone as a daily reminder. And I'll stick that drawing onto my bedroom mirror so I can start the day looking at it. I think that'll be a great way to start the day!"

11

Framework for Working with Boundaries: Identifying Strong and Wobbly Boundaries

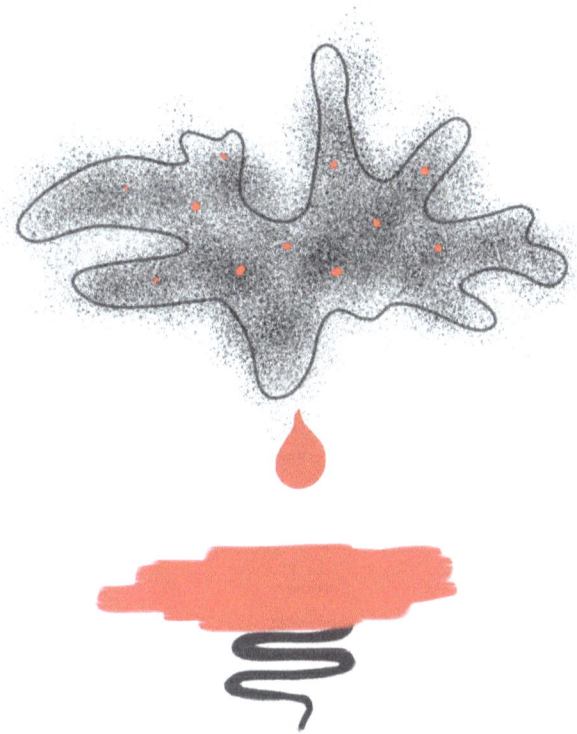

What are boundaries?

Our boundaries are there to keep us safe and help ensure we are aligned with what we value. In a broad sense, boundaries are about influence. By which we mean that we use the power and authority of our boundaries to influence others either appropriately or inappropriately, usually with a lack of awareness of what we are doing.

As practitioners, for example, we are responsible for maintaining our boundaries, and we are all familiar with the boundary of confidentiality. Yet this can be challenged when we are working with an employee but being paid by the employer who may try and engage us to discuss the client without their knowledge. It is important for us to hold our boundaries in such situations. Other boundaries you might be aware of are about the time you give your clients: do you keep within the agreed time or do you give them a bit more? Do you agree to meet outside your desired working hours because they need your help, which perhaps fulfils a need inside you?

As a child, we have no influence over how our boundaries are strengthened or weakened. For instance, if you are constantly told as a child to "be good and behave" in front of other adults, it can send a message to the child that they need to be compliant and that they have no control over their personal space. It can then be hard as an adolescent or adult to say to someone, "Stop, enough is enough," because they have no experience of doing so and it may lead them to do things they don't want to do.

Clear and strong boundaries help people to feel safe and secure, which in turn enables them to be open and honest about their needs and the wants of other people. When a friend asks you to go out in the evening and you really don't want to go, if you had a clear boundary you would be able to share your truth and negotiate an outcome that works for both of you. Our lives, and those of people around us, are greatly simplified by people being more aware of their boundaries and better at maintaining them.

In many more instances, though, we are less aware of our boundaries and manage them with varying degrees of success. The fact that we have not maintained a boundary can be masked by emotions turning inwards, perhaps as frustration due to a desire to assert an opinion but not doing so. Or turned outwards, perhaps as blame. This can create turbulence in a person's inner world and leave them feeling powerless or even open to manipulation.

Our approach

Boundaries represent our principles and values, and we all have strong boundaries in some areas of our lives. One generic boundary we can all probably agree on is that speaking the truth is important. Treating one another with respect – or respectfully – might be another. Fulfilling agreements or doing what you said you would do is probably something we all have an expectation of, as is doing a good day's work for a good day's pay. Strong boundaries are linked to self-esteem and self-worth because of the sense of authenticity and empowerment they generate.

Reaction to somebody testing our boundaries is often felt in the body. People feel it in their stomach, sometimes like a punch. They say their hackles go up, facial expressions change into a frown, or there can be a feeling of anger.

Our approach is to associate clients with their strong boundaries, so they find out more about them and their motivation to keep them in place. There *has* to be a motivation, and it has to result in something positive that empowers the client in some way. It means they have choices about how they treat others and how they want to be treated.

Weak boundaries are very easy to see in others. It's definitely harder to see it in ourselves because we are often in some form of denial

---

However, clients generally do not come to talk about their strong boundaries. But during a session it may become clear that they actually don't have a boundary in place for the topic they are addressing. They may be defensive, feel frustrated with themselves or be inappropriately pointing the finger of blame at other people. We call this a 'wobbly boundary'. Wobbly boundaries give power away to others and can also enable others to manipulate us. When a client's boundary is being breached, they are allowing someone else to do something to them that they don't want and are unable to assert themselves or feel able to control the outcome, or how they respond. This often leads to people participating in things they would rather not be engaged in.

What do we think is generally the root cause of a 'wobbly boundary'?

Behind most 'wobbly boundaries' is fear. Fear of rejection from someone we want respect or love from.

Fear of upsetting the other person. Fear that if we make a fuss, it will have consequences that we don't want to accept or fear of what people will think of us. It could be as simple as accepting an invitation to an event that we don't want to attend. It could be taking on work from a colleague that results in us working extra hours. 'People pleasers' have very wobbly boundaries because their need to be liked, loved and appreciated is stronger than their need to protect themselves.

Fear of the consequences can seem like a reasonable reason to relax boundaries, until you scratch below the surface to consider that they all have a price to pay. Sometimes it seems that giving in is the easier option – "Anything for a quiet life" – but this is a trap. Making it easier for others can mean we are doing ourselves a disservice. We may be swallowing what we want to say, brushing the importance aside mentally, but this is creating cognitive dissonance and internal conflict that often lies unaddressed.

Repeatedly giving up on principles, values and a desire to be authentic can damage a person's self-esteem and contribute to a sense of powerlessness which can be crushing. People may quote examples where others seem to get their needs met and call that selfish or aggressive. But this can be just another way of justifying taking no action.

It is essential to help clients explore what is unconsciously getting in their way from creating or maintaining strong boundaries and consider if the consequences are acceptable.

How might a wobbly boundary show up?

How it can show up for a practitioner

We know that issues concerning boundaries come up frequently in a supervision session. Acknowledging where boundaries exist, identifying where new ones are needed and taking ownership of them are key strategies for strengthening personal and professional boundaries. This ensures our clients can work at their own pace, on their own agenda, without interference or contamination from content that belongs with the practitioner. As an example, a practitioner came to supervision, and it seemed that all of their clients were addressing relationship and marital issues. On investigation it transpired that the practitioner themselves had just come out of a nasty divorce and were projecting their issues into the psyche of their clients and vicariously working through their own unfinished business.

Assuming that the practitioner's wisdom will be helpful to the client can create expectations doomed to failure

When this happens unconsciously it can result in a practitioner inadvertently leading the clients thinking towards outcomes that suit the practitioner's view of the world. When it's done consciously, assumptions that the practitioner's wisdom will be helpful to the client can create expectations doomed to failure.

However, whether we as practitioners like it or not, we do influence our clients because we direct the client's attention through the questions we ask. This is another area where *The ChrisLin Method* helps. As the questions focus specifically on the client's creation and language, it means there is less opportunity for the practitioner to contaminate the content. The *Method* ensures the practitioner is directing attention where it will be helpful for the client rather than because the practitioner is 'interested' or has a view on how things should develop.

It can be helpful to hold a mirror up to yourself and ask:

- What is happening here, and how might I be influencing my client's direction?
- How is this similar to a problem for me, in the past or present?
- Is this saying anything about me and my focus of attention?

How it can show up for a client

A client's language is often an insight into an issue with boundaries. Listen for the following phrases:

- I'm forced to
- I have to
- I don't feel I can say no
- I can't stop it
- I feel frustrated with
- Others expect me to
- I don't have a choice

These are all statements indicating a wobbly boundary.

Feelings of helplessness, annoyance, frustration and blame are energies that can paralyse a client from acting. The question is, do they want to do anything about their wobbly boundary? Sometimes it is easier to stay where they are ('anything for a quiet life') or blame others for their predicament rather than make a choice to challenge what is going on.

The *Boundary Framework* provides an opportunity for the client to explore their boundaries by first examining how they respond from a position of a strong boundary and then reflecting on how different that is compared to a wobbly one. By helping clients find out what is unconsciously influencing their behaviour, they can accept the consequences of doing nothing or take steps to assert a boundary.

Boundary issues come up in all areas of our lives. Here are some examples:

- Parenting: What lines in the sand do you have? Do you know when to say no to your children and mean it, or do you regularly say no but are open to persuasion?
- Rules (for example, house rules regarding smoking and teenagers sleeping together): Does everyone have to help with household tasks?
- Political views and opinions: Can you keep firm boundaries and keep your friendships intact?
- Physical violence, verbal violence or controlling behaviour: Do you have a clear demarcation, or do you, or have you, allowed yourself to be the recipient of inappropriate actions?
- Inconsiderate or uncompassionate actions: Do you do nothing, even when you have an extreme reaction so the people you are with assume you agree with them?
- Work: Do you spend more time at work than you are actually paid for? Do you take on work that should be done by someone else but not say anything about it?

In this chapter's case study, we provide an example of working with a client on boundaries. As mentioned earlier, it is important to recognise that it is a snapshot of the process and not a verbatim account of the whole session. We have endeavoured to select moments where change has taken place to illustrate the flow and use of the *Core Questions* and *Framework Questions* in a real situation.

Engaging further

Book: *Boundaries: When to Say Yes, How to Say No To Take Control of Your Life* by Dr Henry Cloud and Dr John Townsend

Book: *Boundaries for Your Soul: How to Turn Your Overwhelming Thoughts and Feelings into Your Greatest Allies* by Alison Cook and Kimberly Miller

Book: *How to Establish Boundaries: Protect Yourself, Become Assertive, Take Back Control and Set Yourself Free* by Patrick King

Boundary Framework
Creative Process

1. Identify a strong boundary.
   a. Help the client identify a belief, value or concept that they know is very important to them, where they would not allow others to breach it or where they will firmly hold their position. Discuss the qualities of a strong boundary by asking questions such as "What has to be present for you to have a strong boundary?"
2. Invite the client to create an image that represents their strong boundary.
3. It is recommended there is a short break so the client can let go of their strong boundary before moving on to think about their wobbly boundary.
4. Introduce the concept of a wobbly boundary and discuss a situation where the client is unable to maintain their boundaries, and perhaps their values are being stepped upon.
5. Invite the client to create an image that represents their wobbly boundary.
6. Explore the wobbly boundary by selecting questions from *The 9 Core Questions* and *the Framework Questions* below.
   b. Where is the wobble?
   c. Where is your focus drawn to? Tell me more about that.
   d. What does this image get out of being wobbly?
7. Ask the client to put their strong boundary image alongside their wobbly boundary image.
   e. What is the wobbly boundary missing?
   f. What wisdom can the strong boundary give the wobbly boundary?
   h. What needs to happen for the wobbly boundary to become stronger?
   g. In what particular situations does the wobbly boundary need to be stronger?
   i. Knowing what you know now, what needs to happen next?
   j. What will you do differently in future?

As a reminder, it's not necessary to ask all of the questions on every occasion. The case study below demonstrates how we have selected questions from *The 9 Core Questions* and the above list of *Framework Questions* to help the client understand more about themselves and their issue and make a positive shift. As you become familiar with *The ChrisLin Method* you will be able to confidently select questions on the fly as well as adding questions of your own, based on your own intuition.

Introduction to the case study

In this case study we demonstrate how to select questions from *The 9 Core Questions* and the *Framework Questions* so you can see how they work together. We reference the questions as CQ1 for *Core Question 1*, CQ2 for *Core Question 2*, and so on, and FQa, FQb, and so on for questions from the *Framework*.

In addition, we have included an intuitive question that the practitioner asked relying on their own instincts, in the moment, because they sensed it was the right thing to do. It is referenced as IQ.

The specific *Framework Questions* for this topic are:

a. What has to be present for you to have a strong boundary?

b. Where is the wobble?

c. Where is your focus drawn to? Tell me more about that.

d. What does this image get out of being wobbly?

e. What is the wobbly boundary missing?

f. What wisdom can the strong boundary give the wobbly boundary?

g. What needs to happen for the wobbly boundary to become stronger?

h. In what particular situations does the wobbly boundary need to be stronger?

i. Knowing what you know now, what needs to happen next?

j. What will you do differently in future?

Case Study

Background

Jenny was worn out; she was always overwhelmed with the number of things she had to do and the number of people who seemed to depend on her. No matter how much she did and how many people she helped, she always had a never-ending list of things she still needed to get done. This was a pattern both at work and at home. "I feel like I'm going round and round on a hamster wheel and I can't get off. Why can't anyone see I'm overwhelmed and can't take it anymore?" she said.

What would you like to get from the session today?

"To be able to assess what I want to do and be able to say no to the rest. To focus on what I want for myself."

Factors influencing the issue

Being the oldest child with a brother and sister who came five years later, she took on a parenting role. Both her parents worked full time and she noticed early on how her mother ran around before and after work sorting things out and how she sighed a lot. Her memory was mainly of her mother's back as she created a tidy and well-run home. She felt her mum had little patience with her and her siblings. Jenny tried to take some of the burdens off her mother's shoulders. Her mum rewarded her for being helpful by saying, "Mum's little helper, what would I do without you?" This potentially set up a pattern for only feeling validated when she was being helpful.

Exploring the client's creative work

Jenny was reminded that she did not get to the age she is now without having some firm boundaries that she held strongly. Helping her, first of all, to find these strong boundaries was key to working with the wobbly boundaries she was experiencing.

Jenny was asked to think of a situation where she knew that no matter what, she would hold her ground and not be swayed by anyone else. When she expressed a couple of situations, she was asked to pick one and to create an image or metaphor representing her 'strong boundary' and was given 10 minutes to complete her creation. Jenny knew that if anyone criticised her children, she would stand her ground firmly and make it really clear her children were off limits.

Jenny's strong boundary image consisted of an egg shape with a thick line around the perimeter. The egg had some words inside: strong, safe, sure, confident, honest, reliable, committed. In addition, the egg had a little opening or gap in the perimeter.

CQ1: Tell me the story of your image

"I knew I had to draw an oval shape because it feels like it encapsulates everything and keeps all those words safe. It has a little door at the end just in case I want to go outside the boundary or let someone in, but that's completely under my control. No one can get in unless I let them."

From the description Jenny gave, the shift in her body to sit up straight and the tone of her voice, Jenny had got right into being associated with having a strong boundary. We explored the image a bit more using just a few of the Core Questions to support this association.

This activity is about enabling the client to recognise they do have strong boundaries and what happens mentally and physically when they are reacting in line with their values. It is only necessary to spend a few minutes on the image, until the practitioner notices that the client has associated with the sense of a strong boundary.

The next step is to work on the issue the client has brought to the session, or that the practitioner has noticed: the wobbly boundary. We think it is helpful to break the client's train of thought at this point to clear their minds from the strong boundary so they can fully focus on their wobbly boundary. A simple question about how the client arrived today or what the weather is like where they are is often sufficient.

Jenny was asked about how her journey had been that day to help clear her mind so we could introduce the term wobbly boundary and explain what we would do next.

She was asked to think about a time when she felt overwhelmed, stopped thinking about herself and helped others. A time when she couldn't say no.

Jenny was then invited to use her creative materials to represent her 'wobbly boundary' and was given 10 minutes to create her image.

She took a small sponge, dipped it in paint and made splodges in a random way; there were no edges to speak of. It was like a wafting cloud full of holes. In the middle, she drew what looked like tears dripping into a puddle below, and there was a wiggly line coming out of the puddle.

Jenny was asked about her wobbly boundary.

CQ1: Tell me the story of your image

"Well, it looks and feels like an amoeba. It has no backbone and can be blown about in the slightest puff of wind. It feels like it's stuffed with cotton wool or candy floss, but it's not sweet."

CQ2: What does this colour represent to you?

"It's pale and colourless and a bit lifeless. When I look at the image, I feel quite sick and wonder where it came from. It represents just how I feel when I am overwhelmed. I want to paint over it, so I can't see it."

CQ3: What does this shape mean for you? (Pointing to a part of the image that looked like tears.)

"Those little spots of red feel like they have some lifeblood in them. They start in the amoeba, but they have nowhere to go apart from collecting in a deep puddle outside of the lifeless form. Although the spots of colour are small and hardly noticeable, they feel very big to me."

FQb: Where is the wobble in your wobbly boundary?

"Two places, the amoeba and the puddle. I want to put a thick line around the amoeba and give it a bit of a backbone. I don't like the feeling of it. It feels so weak."

Jenny sits back and looks at her image and takes a deep breath in and holds it for a second before breathing out.

Change is beginning to happen! She is beginning to see something she had not noticed before. Jenny picked up her pen and drew a line around the amoeba and made it look more like an egg.

CQ6: What is the relationship between the red part of the image and the puddle?

"What I am seeing is that the red drops are filling up the puddle and the puddle is overflowing. The overflow is just a trickle that eventually just fizzles out. That's strange because the trickle wants to be a flow."

FQc: Where is your focus drawn to? Tell me more about that.

"I'm drawn to the puddle. It seems to be full of feelings and unspoken words. It seems to fill up with thoughts, but they can't escape except by the tiny trickle. But that trickle just fizzles out and dries up. I'm often told that I muddy the waters because I'm not clear. I think that the puddle is the muddy waters because everything gets clogged up in there."

Jenny rested her chin on her hand and was silent while she studied her image and contemplated its meaning.

"That feels a little like what happens to me when I can't say no or say what I want people to do for me. My words dry up; they stay in my head and won't come out. They get stuck. It's like the puddle gets gloopy and holds onto the flow."

CQ7: If that part of your image had a voice, what would it be saying?

"Let me out! Let me say what I think and what I'm feeling. You know that I have wisdom. You need to trust me more, so that you get what you want."

FQd: What does this image get out of being wobbly?

Jenny sat back and took some time to respond.

"Being wobbly means I don't have to make any decisions, I suppose. It's safe, isn't it? People are more likely to like me if I do as they say and do things for them, just like my mum."

Jenny paused and looked down at her image and then glanced up.

"I always thought that if I hadn't helped her, she would never have coped. But, actually, now when I think about it, what I think my mum was doing was just telling me I was a good girl, and it was just her way of saying she loved me."

Jenny was asked to place the strong and wobbly boundary images side by side.

CQ8: What do you know now about your wobbly boundary that you didn't know before?

"The wobbly boundary thinks that it's indispensable and that everything will fall apart if it doesn't do or say what others want to hear. This is how I muddy the waters because people know I'm not happy, but I don't tell them. It already looks better now I have put a boundary around the amoeba, but it's missing strength and clarity and direction. It's missing that little door that has control over what it can say and do, like there is in the strong boundary."

FQf: What wisdom can the strong boundary give the wobbly boundary?

"Speaking out will give both you and others a real sense of who you are, and you will no longer be sitting on the fence. What *you* think and feel is important. I can help you to speak out and be yourself. You don't need to care so much for others all the time. You know what you want to say and do, so make a stand."

FQg: What needs to happen for the wobbly boundary to be stronger?

"It wants to listen to that wisdom. It wants a strong door that gives it choice, so it can decide what it wants to say and do. I want it to be as strong as it is when I defend my children. I can see now what I've brought from my childhood, and I need to let that go. The door will control the flow, so it comes out as strong as it needs to, when it needs to. Like in my strong boundary image. That feels very powerful."

Jenny took a number of pens and added more strength to the egg shape on her wobbly boundary. She changed the muddy water of the puddle into fresh blue water, with a strong flow coming out, and added the words 'speak up for yourself'. The flow had a tap on it so she could control and manage what she said and how she said it.

"I now have a picture I can use to check myself and see if I have the tap on or off. I now need an opportunity to practise it and realise that no one is going to be hurt if I stand my ground. And also, I think I will be respected more if I am able to take better care of myself, which is what my strong boundary does for me. Mmm, that is strange… I no longer have a wobbly boundary, it all appears strong!"

FQh: In what particular situation does the wobbly boundary need to be stronger?

"I have an issue with a friend that I haven't been able to tackle. That's my first place to start."

FQi: Knowing what you know now, what needs to happen next?

"I want to talk to my friend about the support I keep giving her. I need to have a think about what I can give, and when, and let her know. I probably need to be clearer about the effect it's having on me and how I feel so overstretched at the moment. That feels like such a relief. It feels like I have grown up, at least a little!"

FQj: What will you do differently in the future?

"I am determined now to stop people piling things on me and I will stop saying yes all the time. As soon as I get that feeling in my stomach, I will remind myself to step up and be clear about what I can and can't do. Although, I expect it will be hard at first. I also want to be more careful about what I offer to do for other people and be able to draw a line if they demand more than I'm able to do. I now have a door and a tap, and I will use them."

IQ: What do you need to do to ensure you use your door and tap?

"I'm going to use them as a mental image when I do my meditation. I think that's a good way of getting the idea into my life on a regular basis so that I'm reminding myself every day."

As Jenny had found a way to integrate the work into her body and her life, there was no need to go to Step 4, Integration. Instead, Jenny was asked to reflect on what she said she wanted to get from this session.

And when you speak up and tell people what you want, does this enable you to say no, so you can focus on what you want for yourself?

"Yes, I believe so."

Step 5: Closing the session. What needs to happen next with your images?

"I love both of them, but I want to create just one image that tells me where I am now. When I have done that, I'll use it in my meditation and put it on my wall so I can see it every day."

Jenny had reached a new understanding about her wobbly boundary and was content to work on a new image that summed up where she was now and bring it to the next session. This work had created a significant shift in Jenny, and she now felt confident that she could recognise situations where a boundary was involved and be able to assert herself appropriately.

12
Framework for Working with Anger

What is anger?

Anger is one of the emotions all humans experience, along with love, grief and fear, but the intensity of the feeling and people's responses will vary depending on many things: culture, life experiences, nature and nurture. It is, therefore, a natural and normal reaction to situations that individuals find difficult to manage. And like other emotions, people experience anger in various ways, from deep to shallow, significant to minor or benign to toxic.

Descriptions of anger

- Hot and explosive, what we often call 'red anger', which includes fury, rage and fuming.
- Cold and calculating, which we call 'white anger' – a simmering anger never fully expressed. (We know when this is happening when we ask, "Are you okay, is anything wrong?" and they say, "No. I'm fine," with a tone of voice that lets us know they are anything but fine.) Sometimes this is termed passive-aggressive and can be the most challenging anger to deal with because the person feeling it is usually in denial and wants to punish.
- Righteous indignation, often driven by contempt or moral outrage and can be a form of blame.
- Irritation or frustration that comes from trying to stop ourselves from feeling what we really feel.

Anger has an energy that can be frightening to others and even to the person expressing it. They may fear it will take over and that they will do something they regret.

When expressed cleanly and without contamination, anger can energise and motivate us and others. It can help reinforce boundaries and empower us to achieve goals. However, when anger is contaminated with memories of past hurts, it can change our response into something more significant than the event deserves and be a painful experience for all concerned.

If, for example, you kicked me now and I had no residual anger waiting to be expressed, I would be able to say, "I feel really angry that you have kicked me, and I would like you to apologise." In this example the person is acknowledging their anger and what they want the other person to do about it. It is expressed in the moment and at the right 'temperature'. However, if I just exploded with a lot of expletives and a red anger, then my response would be out of kilter with the event that had just taken place. This latter response is likely contaminated with memories from the past about being kicked, hurt or disrespected.

Exploring these past memories is at the core of the *Framework* we share here and involves looking at how, at an unconscious level, the response to a situation in the present is impacted by past life experiences. The aim is to find new ways of dealing with the problem that is proportionate and appropriate to the issue.

Our approach

Anger has a structure. The things that provoke anger are related to a client's beliefs and values, their view of themselves, the world and how it should operate. Things that happened in the past and are unresolved can cause emotions to stack up, waiting for an opportunity to erupt. When this happens, the past contaminates the present, and the client may react inappropriately.

Our approach is to help clients identify the root cause or triggers and provide a way to disconnect the present from the influence of the past. Unpicking the anger reveals that it is made up of many components based on internal thoughts, images or memories, beliefs, values, principles or even projections of the future. Deconstructing the anger into these component parts means the key triggers can be identified. When clients acknowledge the connection between the past and present, they can separate the current event and view it as an independent issue. The anger will then be modified to become appropriate anger or some other response or dissipate altogether.

What do we think is generally the root cause of anger?

We suspect that most anger comes from earlier experiences that were blocked from being expressed, or the child or young person was not listened to or heard.

Two-year-olds know how to have wonderful tantrums. They let us know when something is not right for them. But because parents do not like this form of expression of the child's feelings, they are often shut down. A child who hasn't learnt how to negotiate or communicate what they want without anger or has been continually chastised or repressed from expressing themselves, has this emotion sitting in their soul, waiting for opportunities to come out.

Unfortunately, expressing anger later in life, about something related to earlier feelings, does not solve or deal with the energy buried deep in the psyche. Understanding the root cause and finding a way to learn, understand, and often forgive the incident can neutralise the historic anger as long as the adult is willing to let it go.

How might anger show up?

Anger is an emotion that people find particularly difficult to deal with. Most people do not want to be angry, or like feeling angry. It is rare for clients to say they are raging or furious about something. Rage is a word that most people would deny they feel because it suggests they are out of control. Clients are more likely to express anger, annoyance, frustration or irritation or say they feel uncomfortable about something and may not know why. They may talk about being disappointed that someone has let them down, or they are worried that something they thought was going to happen did not happen. Most people feel that expressing anger is not okay, so they may skirt around what they are really feeling. Taking ownership and accepting the depth of the feeling is a helpful place to start.

There are many things that influence a person's relationship with anger. A client's view of whether anger should be expressed and how it can be expressed may be influenced by their age, gender, upbringing, culture and environment. When this is the case, uncovering the fact that anger is the right emotion to be working on can be tricky. It may even be worth asking a direct question such as, "Would you say the right word for this is anger?" to test it out.

'Red anger' may start with "I feel…." For example: "I feel furious this happened." Or they may say a person is "really frustrating and is driving me mad".

'White anger' is about withholding resources or information. For example, in the workplace, with family members or within friendships: "I'm so annoyed with them that I'm not going to meet them tomorrow." Or, "There's no way I'm going to give them anything now." Or, more subtly, "I'm too busy to talk to them now."

Some clients bottle their anger up, which can result in a great deal of internal conflict that is likely to show up in other ways, physically or emotionally. Or it can manifest as an unexpected outburst.

Someone who is angry can be very frightening, and most of us are willing to do anything to avoid becoming the target of angry conflict. We may even give up our autonomy rather than confront another person's anger. As a result, clients may find ways to distract themselves from taking action and suppress their desire to be authentic.

Examples of situations that can evoke anger

- Kids, not behaving the way that is expected
- Partners, not engaging or contributing what is needed
- Parents, making demands on limited time or resources
- Friends, taking more than they are giving or being needy
- Bosses or colleagues, not listening or understanding your focus of attention
- Neighbours, being difficult about land boundaries, noise, untidiness
- Things not going according to plan, not being able to control what is happening
- Other people not performing or doing what we would want them to do
- Expectations we have of others not being met but not being clear about needs
- Others controlling what we want to do, not sharing or being fair
- Values being violated, cheating, lying, lack of care, doing things that affect another person's wellbeing

In this chapter's case study, we provide an example of working with a client on anger. As mentioned earlier, it is important to recognise that it is a snapshot of the process and not a verbatim account of the whole session. We have endeavoured to select moments where change has taken place to illustrate the flow and use of the *Core Questions* and *Framework Questions* in a real situation.

Engaging further

Book: *The Dance of Connection: How to Talk to Someone When You're Mad, Hurt, Scared, Frustrated, Insulted, Betrayed, or Desperate* by Harriet Lerner

Book: *The Language of Emotions: What Your Feelings Are Trying to Tell You* by Karla McLaren

Book: *Humble Inquiry: The Gentle Art of Asking Instead of Telling* by Edgar Schein

Anger Framework
Creative Process

1. Identify the anger to be worked on.
2. Invite the client to draw a shape that represents the *whole* anger that the client wants to work on. This is called 'anger'. (Or the client may give it a name.)
3. On the same piece of paper (or a separate piece if needed) ask the client to add metaphors or images around anger that represent all its *component* parts. A component part is an element of the whole anger. To find the components ask the client what was going on inside them when they were angry. Stay focused on what the client feels, thinks, says or does. For example: "Part of me was thinking…" or "I'm all churned up inside" or "It made me feel like…." All of these are components.
4. Help the client to explore their anger and its components using a selection from *The 9 Core Questions* and the *Framework Questions* below.
    a. Looking at each component, which of them are influenced by or rooted in a past belief, experience or hurt?
    b. Thinking of those components that are from the past, which component are you drawn to?
    c. Tell me the history of that particular component.
    d. What is this component believing about the current situation?
    e. What does this component need to accept about the situation?
    f. What is this component willing to do now to move the situation forward?
    g. What wisdom or information has this component to offer the whole of anger?

If the client or practitioner realises there is a pattern or common theme to the times they feel angry, the next step may be to work on the pattern or theme itself.

As a reminder, it's not necessary to ask all of the questions on every occasion. The case study below demonstrates how we have selected questions from *The Core Questions* and the above list of *Framework Questions* to help the client understand more about themselves and their issue and make a positive shift. As you become familiar with *The ChrisLin Method* you will be able to confidently select questions on the fly as well as adding questions of your own, based on your own intuition.

Introduction to the case study

In this case study we demonstrate how to select questions from *The 9 Core Questions* and the *Framework Questions* so you can see how they work together. We reference the questions as CQ1 for *Core Question 1*, CQ2 for *Core Question* 2, and so on, and FQa, FQb, and so on for questions from the *Framework*.

The specific *Framework Questions* for this topic are:

a. Looking at each component, which of them are influenced by or rooted in a past belief, experience or hurt?

b. Thinking of those components that are from the past, which component are you drawn to?

c. Tell me the history of that particular component.

d. What is this component believing about the current situation?

e. What does this component need to accept about the situation?

f. What is this component willing to do now to move the situation forward?

g. What wisdom or information has this component to offer the whole of anger?

Case Study

Background

James had real difficulty with people in authority or, in fact, anyone who had a different opinion or who he felt wanted to control him. Consequently, he found it hard to manage his emotions and he was known to be volatile, as he could get angry and lose his temper over what others saw as minor things going wrong. James realised that, usually, one or two people were the target of his anger, which he put down to being sure they were trying to control him. He became intransigent and demanding, making him a nightmare to manage. Although he had lived with outbursts like this for a long time, he was becoming increasingly angry with his growing children as they started to show independence. His wife told him that if he did not sort his anger issue out, she would take the children and leave him. This became his wake-up call. At work, he got feedback that people walked on eggshells around him, which was a total surprise. He said, "Most of the time, I feel like I'm the master of my destiny. I know I'm a bit of a maverick. I like to do things my way, but that makes me successful. Every so often, I just explode because I'm surrounded by idiots, but I'm not like that all the time."

What would you like to get out of the session today?

"I want to be more in control of my emotions, so I handle things better. Most of the time I am calm, and I want more time like that."

Factors influencing the issue

His earliest memories were of a father who would get angry for what appeared to young James to be for nothing in particular. If James did not match up to unspecified rules, his father and mother would withhold food and send him to his room hungry and frustrated. He often did not know what he was being punished for and became very confused. His father's favourite saying was, "You are useless." James often felt "a seething pit of burning bile" in his stomach. At school, he would shout at other kids to get his own way, and this venting released his anger for a short while. This pattern had continued until he sought help. Because his anger was less volatile than his father's, he did not see it as a problem because, until recently, people had just accepted it and said nothing.

Exploring the client's creative work

James was invited to create an image of his anger in the middle of his page. Around it, he was asked to draw symbols or metaphors representing what he was telling himself about this anger.

James created an image of a mountain with a volcano at the top with molten lava spewing over the side, down to what looked like a beach and tranquil sea. Around the outside of the volcano, he created images depicting his internal thoughts about what was happening for him.

CQ1: Tell me the story of your image

"In the centre is the volcano, which seems to be waiting for the next opportunity to spew over. It is never totally dormant. It seems to sneak up on me and erupt without warning."

CQ3: What does this shape mean for you?

"It is a traditional volcano shape, with a crater at the top, and although it has just erupted, it's still full of orange molten lava, and after a while, the crater fills right up again."

CQ6: What is the relationship between the orange lava and the blue colour at the bottom?

"The orange is hot and fiery and seems out of control, whereas the bottom of the mountain is green, and this is a sort of yellow beach. This is the blue sea, and the water is calm. This is all about when things are going well, and everything is calm. The orange and blue are like opposites of one another. The orange is inside the mountain and it's like my passion to achieve things, a burning that keeps me focused. And that is the issue: sometimes it boils over. Everything outside of the volcano is okay and calm."

CQ4: I see that around the edge you have motifs and symbols. What does the size of each component represent?

"They are different sizes because I wanted to represent their importance. They are all about the things that caused me to lose my temper recently. This one is about a person at work. Why would they do that, knowing it makes me mad? This is about my time being wasted. This one is bigger, and it's about betrayal – why would my wife say that to me? This is the biggest one, about the kids. I just want them to have the best future possible, but they are not listening to me. And this represents me. I must be a bad person."

Notice James has listed 5 components: person at work, time being wasted, wife betrayal, kids and himself.

FQa: Looking at each component, which of them are influenced by or rooted in a past belief, experience or hurt?

"That's hard to say because it all feels current. But of course, as I look at the image as a whole, the volcano has been around a long time. And I guess by virtue of that, the mountain must have been around a long time too. Most of the images around the edges feel like they are current. I can see there is a common thread in the pictures about wanting to control all of the situations. Like the person in my team winding me up, and work colleagues wasting my time by asking stupid things. Even my kids, I just want the best for them, and I've always seen it as my job to keep them on the right path."

James paused here to look more at his image and pointed to the component that he labelled as himself.

"I really don't think I'm a bad person, so that component is more of a question or a conclusion from the evidence of the other components. That's quite shocking, to think I'm a bad person from their point of view."

This sounds like an interesting thread to follow but the purpose of this Framework is to help the client discover the root of their anger, so a Framework Question was asked next that presupposes there is a relationship with the past somewhere in the image.

FQb: Thinking of those components that are from the past, which component are you drawn to?

"I'm drawn to the volcano. Well actually, it's the lava, really. I don't like what I'm seeing in front of me. That lava is my anger exploding. I think I've turned into my dad. All of those feelings and thoughts are really related to my dad and how he was with me. He just lost the plot, and I became the target. I'm doing the same, aren't I? Rather than handling it differently. It's like I've learnt nothing from my experience apart from how to punish other people. I think I need some anger management techniques to gain control of myself."

James held his hands up to his face, covering his eyes, like he didn't want to look at his image. Notice how James is starting to take ownership of his behaviour. He's beginning to untangle what belongs to him and what belongs to his father.

FQd: What is the lava believing about the current situation?

"That it has control and is trying to make things better. But when it erupts, it's really destructive, and it probably does exactly the opposite of what I think it does. It doesn't give me more control. It makes others afraid or compliant because they have to be, to protect themselves. I'm living my life doing all the things that were done to me, even though I hated how it made me feel back then. I can see the link between the lava and my own history now."

Notice that James is making sense of his image for himself and gaining new insights.

FQe: What does the lava need to accept about the situation?

"That it needs to get rid of that volcano. The rest of the picture is fine. That volcano is ruining everything. I need to understand that I am not him, and my life is not his life. I want something better. I need to turn that around and find a way of making sure that others see me differently."

As James said he wanted to get rid of the volcano, and wanted others to see him differently, he was asked CQ9 to help him visually represent the change.

CQ9: Is there anything you need to add or take away from the image to represent the change that has happened?

"Yes, I want to put a huge cross through that volcano. In fact, I think I want to draw a whole new picture without a volcano. It doesn't belong with me, and I don't want it to represent me anymore."

James was given some time to recreate his image. It included a green mountain, calm water and a symbol that represented wisdom to him. He said he wanted to be seen as wise and kind.

To conclude, James was asked to reflect on what he said he wanted to get from this session.

Now that you understand what is going on when you get angry, do you sense that you can be more in control of your emotions and handle things better, and be calm?

"I have a way to go, but I now know what I need to work on, and that I can get help. I need to make this happen. I need to think more about the consequences. I already feel halfway there. I want people to feel relaxed around me and think of me as a good person so people can approach me and challenge me if they want to."

James had really worked hard in this session to uncover what was in his unconscious that was driving his behaviour. He made a connection with his past, and how he was mirroring the behaviour of his father to some extent. He recognised for himself that there would be additional work for him to do in the future. This is a good place to leave James; he's not ready to go to Step 4 and Step 5: Integration and Closing the Work. So, in the next sessions, James worked further on his new image to uncover what specific changes would occur in his beliefs and behaviours and worked separately on coming to a resolution regarding his relationship with his father. Only then was James ready to move on to Step 4 and Step 5.

Afterword

Writing this book has been both a hard slog at times and a labour of love. Initially, we only had a vague idea of what we wanted to convey to our readers. But we trusted that as we started to write, the words would flow, and the book would take on a life of its own. And it has.

We both believed we had something unique to offer in the arena of working creatively because of the positive feedback we had received from clients, workshop participants and trainees over the years. And now that we have completed the book, we are even more certain that what we offer is worthwhile and fulfils our value to 'make a difference' in the world.

Throughout the year it has taken to write this book, we discovered even more about what we do when we work creatively with people. At the start, we didn't fully appreciate how much structure we had developed, but not committed to paper. Nor had we realised how important some of the things were that we naturally did as an integral part of working with clients. For example, *The 5 Steps* were already there, but we had not realised that until we started to dig deeper into what we actually did, so we could articulate it in this book. We can remember a feeling of great satisfaction when we realised there was already a structure, and we just had to name it.

Becoming authors has also helped us clarify how much joy we gain from teaching what we know. We love to share the things we have discovered, and we hope we have passed on both our joy and also our *Method* in a way that makes it possible for others to follow and develop different ways of working creatively. We also take great pride in knowing that our trainees and workshop participants have noticed the post-book development, and we would like to thank you for being part of our journey.

We hope we have inspired you to work creatively and be curious about all the resources in this book, and elsewhere, so you can develop a style that works for you. We look forward to seeing you in our workshops and training courses in the future, and thank you in advance for recommending our book to others.

We want to close the book by paying tribute to one another and by acknowledging the contributions we have each made to the project. As anyone who has met us knows, we are very different people, and our thinking styles are in many ways opposite. But we know that, without the other, this book would never have seen the light of day. It is our differences as well as our similarities that have been our strength and the key that has unlocked the creativity that has become this book.

If you would like to know more about us, our workshops or training in *The ChrisLin Method* or would like to invite us to run experiential events for your group, please take a look at our website and reach out to us at **www.awakeningcreativity.co.uk**.

Bibliography

Barnes, A. (2022). *The Anxiety Workbook: Practical Tips and Guided Exercises to Help You Overcome Anxiety*. Summersdale Publishers Ltd.

Bettelheim, B. (2010). *The Uses of Enchantment: The Meaning and Importance of Fairy Tales*. Vintage.

Cameron, J. (2016). *The Artist's Way: 30th Anniversary Edition*. Penguin.

Cloud, H., & Townsend, J. (2017). *Boundaries Updated and Expanded Edition: When to Say Yes, How to Say No To Take Control of Your Life*. Zondervan.

Cook, A., & Miller, K. (2018). *Boundaries for Your Soul: How to Turn Your Overwhelming Thoughts and Feelings into Your Greatest Allies*. Thomas Nelson.

Dryden, W. (2020). *Ten Steps to Positive Living*. Hachette UK.

Dyer, W. W. (2009). *Stop The Excuses! How To Change Lifelong Thoughts*. Hay House.

Edwards, B. (2012). *Drawing on the Right Side of the Brain: The Definitive, 4th Edition*. Penguin.

Flowers, B. S., Scharmer, C. O., Jaworski, J., & Senge, P. M. (2011). *Presence: Exploring Profound Change in People, Organizations and Society*. Hachette UK.

Jeffers, S. (2014). *Feel The Fear and Do It Anyway*. Random House.

Johnson, R. A. (2009). *Inner Work: Using Dreams and Active Imagination for Personal Growth*. Harper Collins.

Kimberley, K. (2022). *Thinking Like Magic: Transform your Mental Wellbeing using CBT Techniques*. Bookboon. https://bookboon.com

King, P. (2020). *How to Establish Boundaries: Protect Yourself, Become Assertive, Take Back Control, and Set Yourself Free*. PKCS Media.

Krystal, P. (2019). *Cutting the Ties that Bind: Growing Up and Moving On (First revised edition)*. Sheema Medien Verlag.

Lawley, J., & Tompkins, P. (2000). *Metaphors in Mind: Transformation Through Symbolic Modelling*. Crown House Pub Limited.

LeBoon, R. (2018). *Rethinking Intuition: Using the Framework of an Integrative-Brain Assessment for Optimal Decision-Making. Master of Philosophy in Organizational Dynamics Theses. 13*. https://repository.upenn.edu/od_theses_mp/13

Lerner, H. (2009). *The Dance of Connection: How to Talk to Someone When You're Mad, Hurt, Scared, Frustrated, Insulted, Betrayed, or Desperate*. Harper Collins.

Lewis, T., Amini, F., & Lannon, R. (2007). *A General Theory of Love*. Vintage.

Malchiodi, C. (2007). *The Art Therapy Sourcebook*. McGraw Hill Professional.

McLaren, K. (2010). *The Language of Emotions: What Your Feelings Are Trying to Tell You*. Sounds True.

Moon, B.L. (2002). *Working with Images: The Art of Art Therapists*. Charles C Thomas Publisher.

Owen, N. (2004). *More Magic of Metaphor: Stories for Leaders, Influencers, Motivators and Spiral Dynamics Wizards*. Crown House Publishing.

Parsons, L., & Freed, J. (2012). *Right-Brained Children in a Left-Brained World: Unlocking the Potential of Your ADD Child*. Simon and Schuster.

Pearson, C. S. (2012). *Awakening the Heroes Within: Twelve Archetypes to Help Us Find Ourselves and Transform Our World*. Harper Collins.

Pink, D. H. (2010). *Drive: The Surprising Truth About What Motivates Us*. Canongate Books.

Schein, E. H., & Schein, P. A. (2021). *Humble Inquiry, Second Edition: The Gentle Art of Asking Instead of Telling*. National Geographic Books.

Stanton, P. (2019). *Conscious Creativity: Look, Connect, Create*. Leaping Hare Press.

Strozzi-Heckler, R. (2014). *The Art of Somatic Coaching: Embodying Skillful Action, Wisdom, and Compassion.* North Atlantic Books.

Tolle, E. (2010). *The Power of Now: A Guide to Spiritual Enlightenment.* New World Library.

Van der Kolk, B. (2014). *The Body Keeps the Score: Mind, Brain and Body in the Transformation of Trauma.* Penguin UK.

References

Introduction

Albert Einstein, physicist. Letter to Carl Seelig, his biographer, March 11, 1952. Einstein Archive 39-013. A similar sentiment was expressed in a letter to Hans Muehsam, March 4, 1953, Einstein Archive 38-424

Carl Jung, psychiatrist and psychologist. Carl Jung, *Aion Christ: A Symbol of the Self*, pp. 70-71, para. 126.

Book: Tolle, E. (2010). *The Power of Now: A Guide to Spiritual Enlightenment*. New World Library.

Book: Malchiodi, C. (2007). *The Art Therapy Sourcebook*. McGraw Hill Professional.

Chapter 1

Ananda K Coomaraswamy was a renowned philosopher of Indian art who interpreted and introduced Indian art to the West. Book: Coomaraswamy, A.K. (1934). *The Transformation of Nature in Art*. Dover Publications.

The American Art Therapy Association. Access to their bibliography: https://arttherapy.org

Carl Jung, psychiatrist and psychologist. Book: Jung, C. G. (1966). *The Spirit in Man, Art and Literature* (R.F.C Hull, Trans.). Pantheon Books.

Book: Stanton, P. (2019). *Conscious Creativity: Look, Connect, Create*. Leaping Hare Press.

Chapter 2

Lisa D Hinz is an Associate Professor of Art Therapy and Director of Art Therapy at Dominican University of California and teaches in the therapeutic uses of art and the Expressive Therapies Continuum (ETC).

Book: Hinz, L.D. (2019). *Expressive Therapies Continuum: A Framework for Using Art Therapy* (2nd edition). Routledge.

Book: Lawley, J., & Tompkins, P. (2000). *Metaphors in Mind: Transformation Through Symbolic Modelling*. Crown House Publishing Limited.

Chapter 3

Robert Bresson was a French painter, screenwriter and film director. https://thecitesite.com/authors/robert-bresson

Book: Edwards, B. (2012). *Drawing on the Right Side of the Brain: The Definitive, 4th Edition*. Penguin.

Book: Flowers, B. S., Scharmer, C. O., Jaworski, J., & Senge, P. M. (2011). *Presence: Exploring Profound Change in People, Organizations and Society*. Hachette UK.

Chapter 4

Enrich Fromm, social psychologist and philosopher, known for his books on human nature, society and love and as a critic of Sigmund Freud.

Clean Language is a set of questions developed by David J Grove. The questions focus on the symbols and metaphors that people use. It is also the basis of Symbolic Modelling, a stand-alone method and process for psychotherapy and coaching developed by James Lawley and Penny Tompkins. Clean Learning is a training provider https://cleanlearning.co.uk

'Sticks and Stones' proverb first recorded in *The Christian Recorder* (Philadelphia, Pennsylvania, USA) on March 22, 1862. https://en.wikipedia.org/wiki/Sticks_and_Stones

Book: Owen, N. (2004). *More Magic of Metaphor: Stories for Leaders, Influencers, Motivators and Spiral Dynamics Wizards*. Crown House Publishing.

Book: Bettelheim, B. (2010). *The Uses of Enchantment: The Meaning and Importance of Fairy Tales*. Vintage.

References

Chapter 5

Henri Matisse, renowned painter, draughtsman, printmaker and sculptor famous as the leader of the Fauvist art movement and pursued the expressiveness of colour throughout his career.

Book: Moon, B.L. (2002). *Working with Images: The Art of Art Therapists*. Charles C Thomas Publisher

Book: Cameron, J. (2016). *The Artist's Way: 30th Anniversary Edition*. Penguin.

Chapter 6

Stephen R Covey, educator, author, businessman and keynote speaker. He is credited for writing one of the most influential business books of the twentieth century. Covey, S. R. (2020). *The Seven Habits of Highly Effective People*. Simon and Schuster.

Book: Van der Kolk, B. (2014). *The Body Keeps the Score: Mind, Brain and Body in the Transformation of Trauma*. Penguin UK.

Book: Strozzi-Heckler, R. (2014). *The Art of Somatic Coaching: Embodying Skillful Action, Wisdom, and Compassion*. North Atlantic Books.

Book: Pearson, C. S. (2012). *Awakening the Heroes Within: Twelve Archetypes to Help Us Find Ourselves and Transform Our World*. Harper Collins.

Chapter 7

Maya Angelou was an American memoirist, popular poet and civil rights activist who died in 2014. Maya Angelou Quotes. BrainyQuote.com, BrainyMedia Inc, 2023. https://www.brainyquote.com/quotes/maya_angelou_101310, accessed March 16, 2023.

Edward De Bono, a leading author and authority in the field of creative thinking, originator of the term Lateral Thinking and descriptor of the mind as a self-organising system.
Book: De Bono, E. (2009). *Lateral Thinking: A Textbook of Creativity*. Penguin UK.
Book: De Bono, E. (2016). *Six Thinking Hats*. Penguin Books Limited.

Book: Krystal, P. (2019). *Cutting the Ties that Bind: Growing Up and Moving On (First revised edition)*. Sheema Medien Verlag.

Book: Dyer, W. W. (2009). *Stop The Excuses! How To Change Lifelong Thoughts*. Hay House UK Ltd.

Chapter 9

Carl Jung quote, found in a short letter, written in 1916 in response to Fanny Bowditch. https://www.angelikiyiassemides.com/en/news/misusing-jung-who-looks-outside-dreams-who-looks-inside-awakes

Chapter 10

The Fight/Flight response was developed by Walter Bradford Cannon, an American neurologist and physiologist who used the word homeostasis to describe the body's desire to achieve equilibrium. https://en.wikipedia.org/wiki/Fight-or-flight_response

The quotations regarding the difference between anxiety and fear: Thierry Steimer.
Steimer, T. (2022). The biology of fear-and anxiety-related behaviors. *Dialogues in clinical neuroscience*.

Book: Barnes, A. (2022). *The Anxiety Workbook: Practical Tips and Guided Exercises to Help You Overcome Anxiety*. Summersdale Publishers Ltd.

Book: Kimberley, K. (2022). *Thinking Like Magic: Transform Your Mental Wellbeing using CBT Techniques*. Bookboon https://bookboon.com

Chapter 11

Book: Cloud, H., & Townsend, J. (2017). *Boundaries: Updated and Expanded Edition: When to Say Yes, How to Say No To Take Control of Your Life*. Zondervan.

Book: Cook, A., & Miller, K. (2018). *Boundaries for Your Soul: How to Turn Your Overwhelming Thoughts and Feelings into Your Greatest Allies*. Thomas Nelson.

Book: King, P. (2020). *How to Establish Boundaries: Protect Yourself, Become Assertive, Take Back Control, and Set Yourself Free.* PKCS Media.

Chapter 12

Book: Lerner, H. (2009). *The Dance of Connection: How to Talk to Someone When You're Mad, Hurt, Scared, Frustrated, Insulted, Betrayed, or Desperate.* Harper Collins.

Book: McLaren, K. (2010). *The Language of Emotions: What Your Feelings Are Trying to Tell You.* Sounds True.

Book: Schein, E. H., & Schein, P. A. (2021). *Humble Inquiry, Second Edition: The Gentle Art of Asking Instead of Telling.* National Geographic Books

Further Resources

Introduction

Below we share a number of practical resources that we think are helpful for anyone aspiring to work creatively with clients.

The Anatomy of Loneliness: How to Find Your Way Back to Connection	Teal Swan
Archetype Cards	Caroline Myss
The Artist's Way	Julia Cameron
The Art Therapy Source Book	Cathy A Malchiodi
Becoming: A Guided Journal of Discovering Your Voice	Michelle Obama
Boundaries for Your Soul	Alison Cook
Boundaries, Updated and Expanded: When to Say Yes and How to Say No	John Townsend
The Complete Dictionary of Symbols	Jack Tresidder
Conscious Creativity: Look, Connect, Create	Philippa Stanton
Ditching the Imposter Syndrome	Clare Josa
Drawing on the Right Side of the Brain	Betty Edwards
The Dreaming Source of Creativity	Amy Mindell
Escaping Toxic Guilt	Susan Carrell
Finding Joy in Loneliness	Brittani Krebbs
Four Steps to Forgiveness	William Fergus Martin

Guilt Shame and Anxiety: Understanding and Overcoming Negative Emotions	Peter R. Breggin
Healing the Shame	John Bradshaw
How to Establish Boundaries: Protect Yourself, Become Assertive, Take Back Control and Set Yourself Free	Patrick King
How To Let Go of Guilt and Regret and Forgive Yourself	Stephanie Workman
Let Go of the Guilt	Valorie Burton
The Madness of Grief	Rev. Richard Coles
The Magic of Metaphor	Nick Owen
Metaphors in Mind: Transformation through Symbolic Modelling	Penny Tompkins and James Lawley
Overcoming Regret	Carole Klein
The Power of Now	Eckhart Tolle
Right-Brained Children in a Left-Brained World	Jeffrey Freed and Laurie Parsons
Shame & Guilt: Masters of Disguise	Jane Middleton-Moz
Thinking Like Magic: Transform your Mental Wellbeing using CBT techniques	Karen Kimberley
Together: The Healing Power of Human Connection in a Sometimes Lonely World	Vivek H Murthy
Unfuck your Boundaries: Build Better Relationships Through Consent	Faith G Harper

Models and theories

Clean Language

Clean Language is a simple set of questions developed by counselling psychologist David Grove. These questions are used with a person's own words to direct their attention to some aspect of their own experience. https://cleanlearning.co.uk

NLP

NLP helps people to better understand the way their brain processes the words they use and how that can impact their past, present and future. https://anlp.org/knowledge-base/definition-of-nlp

Art therapy

www.baat.org/About-Art-Therapy

Humanistic psychology – Carl Rogers

www.eln.co.uk/blog/humanistic-theory-by-psychologist-carl-rogers

https://ahpp.org.uk

Gestalt Theory

http://gpti.org.uk

https://gestaltcentre.org.uk

Neuroscience psychology/cognitive psychology

This is a more in-depth study that deals with how biological and chemical processes make the brain and nervous system function. www.bna.org.uk

CBT

Almost all people have one or more of these core beliefs: I'm stupid, I'm a failure, I'm unlovable. Three common challenges to the client's thinking: Is the thinking True? Is it Real? Is it Helpful? www.psychologytools.com/self-help/what-is-cbt

Videos

Awakening creativity – Self Sabotage – full client session

https://youtu.be/fWf2ltAtERI

Awakening creativity – A coach's perspective in the use of creativity in her practice
https://youtu.be/y78bMN8O1CE

Awakening creativity – Working with Boundaries – full client session
https://youtu.be/1Z-OCYs7Gvk

Brené Brown: The power of vulnerability
https://www.youtube.com/watch?v=iCvmsMzlF7o

Brené Brown: Listening to Shame
https://www.ted.com/talks/brene_brown_listening_to_shame?language=en

Brené Brown on Empathy
https://www.youtube.com/watch?v=1Evwgu369Jw

Kristen Neff on Self-compassion
https://www.youtube.com/watch?v=MEyJ_H1U5SQ

Acknowledgments

We want to thank many people for making this book possible. At the forefront of our minds are the many practitioners and clients who have been willing to explore and experiment with us as we have been developing what we now call *The ChrisLin Method*.

Thank you to all our friends who, when we shared our intention to write a book on working creatively with clients, were excited, patient and supportive, especially when we went through the doldrums and were not sure how to move things forward.

We'd like to thank ….

Christina's daughter, Siobhan, and Lindsey's son, Christian, who we think have always been a bit mystified about what we do and are, nonetheless, proud that we are finally becoming authors.

Lindsey's husband, Mark, for his unfailing love and support.

Penny Tompkins, who continued to support us during our exploration when we changed from face-to-face to online workshops and shared many valuable thoughts and ideas to help us move forward with the project. She has been relentlessly generous in discussing her approach to Clean Language, and Christina will always be grateful for her constant loving friendship.

John Wilson, Sandra Wilson and Fabienne Chazeaux, for welcoming us to their Onlinevents.co.uk platform and encouraging us to share our knowledge and providing an opportunity to work with many practitioners worldwide.

Fiona Eaton, who has continued to inspire us with her approach to creative work after completing *The ChrisLin Method* training course.

Christian Scott, who has created the internal images for the book that so beautifully represent our work.

Lucy Harris, who has created the amazing image for our front cover.

Katariina Jarvinen, our photographer, who provided our professional headshots.

Our proofreaders and reviewers, Amanda Bouch, Anna Gordon, Carey Davidson, David Lines, Karen Kimberley and Shirley Collier, who have read our manuscript and given us helpful and encouraging feedback. And especially Benson Inkley and Fiona Eaton for their many contributions.

Jo Parfitt, Jack Scott and Paddy Hartnett and the team at Springtime Publishing who have been holding our hands every step of the way through the publishing process to make this book the best it can be.

About the Authors

Our journey to creativity

As anyone who has met us knows, we couldn't be more different. Christina has a background filled with a lifetime of counselling and coaching experience, while Lindsey came to coaching after a career in sales and HR in the technology sector. How, then, do we make such a good pair? It is because we complement each other. And, importantly, we have the same goal: to share what we know and expand the use of creativity as a therapeutic technique because we both believe in its value.

We are lucky that we think differently in almost all aspects because it makes us stronger, and we have built up huge regard and trust in one another. This means we can challenge each other, as and when the need arises, and remain the best of friends and make the best decisions based on our joint goal. Together we test and trial ideas through very different lenses, which we feel brings a valuable robustness to our work.

Christina's journey

Growing up in Ireland, the daughter of a Psychoanalyst who was himself a member of the 'Monkstown Group' – the renowned psychoanalytical community in Dublin led by 'Jonty' Jonathan Hanahan – it's perhaps unsurprising that Christina followed in her father's footsteps. With a liberal parenting approach and a home regularly filled with the leading psychoanalysts of the time who were actively engaged in pushing the barriers of psychoanalysis, Christina will have unknowingly absorbed the importance of working with the mind and helping people live more fulfilling lives.

Although not consciously aware of this early influence, Christina's career path led her to attend teacher-training college, where she became a group worker for young people who were non-school attendees. This role proved a turning point as she realised how fulfilling it was to help youngsters who were, and felt, disadvantaged in life to learn to be filled with choices and possibilities.

Creativity became her go-to approach for helping them express themselves. Many were non-readers and not very articulate, so she introduced creativity, initially in the form of colouring-in books. She discovered that as they became absorbed in colouring an image, they started to talk and would answer her questions, and she witnessed a physical and mental change taking place in them. She recognised that they were digging deep into their inner world and gaining an understanding of themselves.

In the decades that followed, Christina qualified in Humanistic Psychology and later went on to teach the course at Surrey University as well as teach counselling skills at Reading University. She became, amongst other things, an NLP Master Trainer and facilitated courses based on John Heron's work, including the 6 Category Intervention Analysis. By the mid-80s, Christina was working with organisations where she offered creativity as a way of developing trust in teams, building strategies for open, honest conversations and constructively challenging one another. Amongst other things, she also ran her own 'Creating from the Soul' retreats for personal development using art therapy, became a coach supervisor and today she continues to work as a supervisor and run her own private practice.

Christina's professional career has been threaded with creativity that has benefited many hundreds of clients. She firmly believes that helping clients to create something outside of themselves, from their inner mind, in the form of a metaphor or symbol, means that the unconscious is free to do its work so that real change can take place. It is her broad and deep knowledge, experience and insight, that she shares with you in this book, that has made *The ChrisLin Method* what it is today.

Lindsey's journey

Creativity in its broadest sense has always been a thread in Lindsey's life, from her early years with art and dance to her corporate career, where she was lucky enough to see the power of metaphors when used in training to help derive meaning, generate mutual understanding and promote safe debate within teams.

However, it was a fortunate turn in her career in the late 1990s and a move into Organisational Development and training that helped her realise her calling was to work more deeply with people. In particular she wanted a more specific involvement in their personal development, and this career change led to qualifying as an NLP Practitioner. Since then, she has become CIPD qualified and trained in many models, systems and techniques, including approaches such as Clean Language, Transactional Analysis, Person-Centred

Therapy, CBT, Motivational Interviewing and models by Nancy Kline and Kristin Neff, to name a few. But still, something was missing.

Meeting Christina allowed her to connect her former creative approaches, her knowledge of developing systemic processes and her coaching skills to co-develop *The ChrisLin Method*. Her curiosity has led to a greater understanding of the human condition, and she has been highly influenced by people such as Bessel van der Kolk, Peter Levine and Stephen Porges. She firmly believes that working creatively enables deep and lasting change to occur by providing a unique opportunity to uncover the hidden, unconscious thoughts that so heavily influence a person's behaviour. She is immensely proud of the work she and Christina have achieved in developing and documenting a repeatable Method that means other practitioners can easily adopt creativity, and in doing so, make an even greater impact on the lives of clients around the world.

www.ingramcontent.com/pod-product-compliance
Lightning Source LLC
Chambersburg PA
CBHW051331110526
44590CB00032B/4479